BARBARA KYNE

A CRACK IN THE WORLD

Cofounders: Taj Forer and Michael Itkoff
Creative Director: Ursula Damm
Copy editor: Elizabeth Bell
Editorial Assistant: Dasha Kabanova

ISBN 978-1-942084-20-4

Printed in China

Daylight Books
E-mail: info@daylightbooks.org
Web: www.daylightbooks.org

To my Fran, as always.

SOMETHING IN THE TREES, AN INTRODUCTION

I know a bank where the wild thyme blows / Where oxlips and the nodding violet grows,
Quite over-canopied with luscious woodbine / With sweet musk-roses, and with eglantine.

—William Shakespeare, *A Midsummer Night's Dream*

Light. This is her focus. Not just where the camera is aimed, but where her mind has turned.

If I find myself asking how long Barbara Kyne has been looking in this direction, it is because I know she has focused on this subject before. This extraordinary collection was preceded by a slim book appropriately named *By Fire*, containing black-and-white photographs that depict a campfire, its flames, the sparks that rise in the air around it, the glow. There is one figure here too, at the edge of the real action, but fading into a soft focus, she does not draw the eyes. What does fascinate, thrill, marvel is the dance of sparks, the spreading glow, and in one dramatic photograph, the flames themselves, which appear as a dense, even viscous, intense species of light.

As has been pointed out countless times by now, a photograph is not and can never be a simple record of reality. Like a painting or a drawing, each photographic image mirrors the perspective, frame of mind, interests, and sensibilities of the photographer. Even when, as with a scientific regimen or bureaucratic requirements, the focus and framing have been directed by institutions, the images produced will reflect the ideas and prejudices of those commanding agencies. Photographs taken of prisoners who have been booked by police, for instance, tell as much about our society as they do about anyone accused of a criminal act.

But of course the reverberations do not stop with the photographer. The way each of us responds also tells us something about ourselves. So I find myself asking, what is it in the photographs in *this* book that moves me so

deeply? That they are beautiful goes without saying. But I know something else here. A reflection of an experience I have had all my life.

The phenomenon has been relegated to the fringe of any shared awareness for so long that it remains nameless. If you have experienced it, you may have said to yourself, as I have at times, that this unnamed dimension is just another aspect of beauty. I might say it is subtle, lingering at the edges of awareness. But paradoxically, it is also quite vivid. Even vital.

And why should this vitality be surprising, after all? The subjects of many of Kyne's photographs—trees, grass, scrubs, plants—are alive. Many of us have also come to understand that soil is alive too. Yes, yes. But still, I sense there is something more. Evident and elusive. Something internal occurring in the trees, the plants, the stars in the night sky, that seduces me, draws me in toward these images and at the same time inward toward a lesser-known territory in myself.

As I search this territory, I find myself thinking of the way light is portrayed in the later work of Rembrandt. After many years as a celebrated portrait painter, he departed from the convention of portraiture in the 17th century, which was to depict the subject in an evenly distributed light, and instead painted in the shadows and brighter lights he saw falling here and there on his canvases. Thus light itself became as much a subject as those who posed for him. Two hundred years later, impressionist painters began to inquire into the nature of light itself, how a landscape changed at different seasons or different times of day, how light creates colors that the human eye mixes. But these photographs take the venture even further. Here, I feel as if I am meeting light as being, as a force. A force that if it is not entirely mysterious, is still a marvel, wondrous.

I am reminded here of the Cottingley Faeries, a series of photographs taken by two Victorian girls, Elsie Wright and Frances Griffiths, at the dawn of the 20th century. Supposedly documenting meetings the girls claimed they had had with fairies, at the time they were made, these obvious fakes were wildly popular, fooling even Arthur Conan Doyle, though one suspects he wanted to be fooled. Despite the highly logical character of his creation, Sherlock Holmes, Doyle was drawn to mysticism, as were a surprising number of Victorians.

I can easily imagine why. This was the period in which industrialization had finally triumphed, and with that victory a mechanistic view of the universe transformed the way we see. The material world, once a fairyland with an intrinsic magic, had become disenchanted. By the 19th century, the triumph of science had produced mechanical miracles, ones that could be explained, predicted, and controlled.

The ensuing loss of any deeper meaning was lamented by many, including the Romantic poet Wordsworth, who argued, "our meddling intellect / mis-shapes the beauteous forms of things: / We murder to dissect." Still, whether moved by a "host of daffodils" or touched by the sunrise he saw from Westminster Bridge in 1802, for Wordsworth, nature remained a powerful teacher, instructing through splendor.

Surely it is a kindred wisdom that is captured in the photographs collected here. My first response was a quick intake of breath. And then "Oh"—not just as an expression of admiration but as recognition. Yes, yes, *here* it *is.* That vitality. Not *how* light affects the growth of plants, the soil, the atmosphere, as science explains to us, but the deeper dimensions of the presence of light. Shimmering, magical, even if explained by formulae, marvelous, a series of daily wonders, transformations taking place all around us and, eventually, inside us.

I am not speaking of faeries, or illusions, or metaphors here. Many religious traditions, including Christianity, Judaism, Islam, and Buddhism, have used sparks or beams of light as symbols of divine energy, and Babylonian, Greek, and Roman myths place solar and lunar gods and goddesses in their pantheons. But, both in human history and in each of our lives, the direct experience of light precedes any myth or metaphor. Not just light from above, but light that dwells on earth. Incorporated into soil, plants, trees, sunlight becomes an intimate companion. Of course, we know from Western science that by a process known as photosynthesis, the energy of light becomes part of the body of a leaf, a branch, a petal, a shaft of wheat, and, through what we eat, ourselves.

But knowing *how* something happens is not always to fully take in *what* happens. The error arises, of course, in a habit of mind engrained in us over centuries, which, by dividing spirit from nature, excises the effect any such exchange has on the soul. So the utter intimacy of light can easily elude us. Or, if we feel the thrill of an exchange, a relationship, even a union, quick and brightening, often joyous, we have no words to give it. And so it becomes easy not only to forget but to deny the existence of this connection.

What Kyne's photographs capture is, among many things, the experience of light as a bond. As the medium that binds together all the creatures in a meadow or on a forest floor, for instance, a bonding that occurs not only between shrubs and root and trees and grass and flowers but also between us, human beings, and all that we witness, including, as we gaze up at the night sky, the stars above us, framed by the silhouettes of tree branches.

But this bonding carries another understanding that perhaps our culture has not equipped us to accept. Thus we often treat the act of seeing as a kind of triumph over nature, evidence of our singular power, our capacity to control other creatures, the weather, the earth, and thus our own fates. So, looking at the dried brambles of a plant—is it ceanothus, sage, soap root, lupine, buckeye, manzanita? one can't tell in this dried form—we see death. But when we separate ourselves from this scene and forget the bond we experienced, we can also leave behind the sure sensation that we too will one day die, and that this is inevitable, a fate we cannot control.

Kyne's camera sees past that illusion. Indeed, through at least one of her frames, imbued with a hazy, lethargic, yellowish, almost heavy light, we are invited to enter the world of the dead, a world that belongs to us, too, with which, despite all our attempts at denial, we are well familiar.

But if we have lost a comforting illusion, through these images we gain (or in fact *regain*) a great deal more. We are no longer in a meaningless void. Nor are we isolated in the act of seeing. All knowledge is the result of collaboration. This is true on the simplest level of the senses. With seeing, for example, which is the subject here, it is not just our ability to see that creates vision but the fact that due to the material properties of earthly existence, what we are seeing is visible. And in the act of collaboration, we are also participating, taking part in, have become part of all that lives and dies. In this newly constituted vision of the world, meaning is neither beyond us nor lost, but enters and seduces us, is ingested, inhaled, taken in, seen, and shared as an ontological commons, like the light that informs these photographs, the medium in which we all swim and thrive.

And there is this, too: If these photographs are grounded, at the same time, they expand our perception. To be grounded does not mean, as is

too often assumed in Western culture, lacking in imagination. I am thinking now of Pacific coast Native American mythology, in which the world was created by the sun god Kodoyanpe in collaboration with the trickster Coyote. Kyne invites the trickster into her process, while, as she describes it, she breaks "the rules of craft in order to come up with things" that she has not seen before. And while she does this, she often finds "a crack in the world" where other layers appear, what she also calls a crack in "the normal."

Her words remind me of quotations I read recently from a statement by the artist and sculptor Eva Hesse about the way she works. In one place she declares that she would like her work "to go beyond" her own "preconceptions," and in another, she tells us, "It is my main concern to go beyond what I know and what I can know."[1]

Isn't this what we need now in a world filled with belligerent certainties? The capacity to wait and see, to take in, the willingness to recognize and acknowledge the presence of other dimensions containing more than we know or can know, is present not only in the methodology used to make these images but in the effect they have on those who see them. "We can't know as much about dirt as the grass does," Kyne writes, but through her beautiful work, we can glimpse the depth of what we do not know, and that makes all the difference.

Susan Griffin
Berkeley, California, 2016

---

1 From a statement by Eva Hesse for Hesse's installation *Chain Polymers*, quoted by Carol Ann Davis in her essay "Eva Hesse Material," *American Poetry Review*, November/December 2015, Vol. 44, Issue 6.

We are stardust
We are golden
And we've got to get ourselves
Back to the garden

Joni Mitchell, *Woodstock*

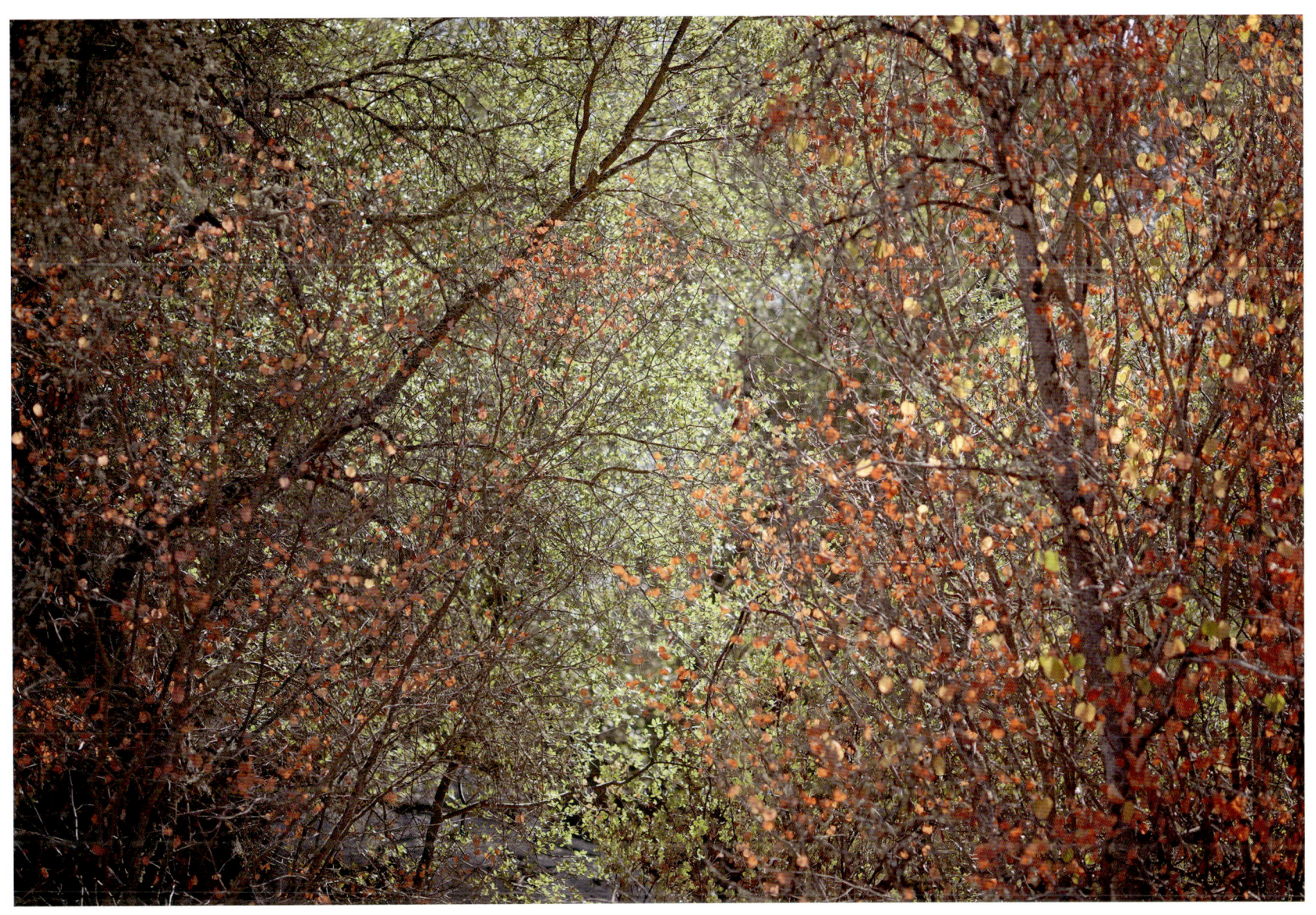

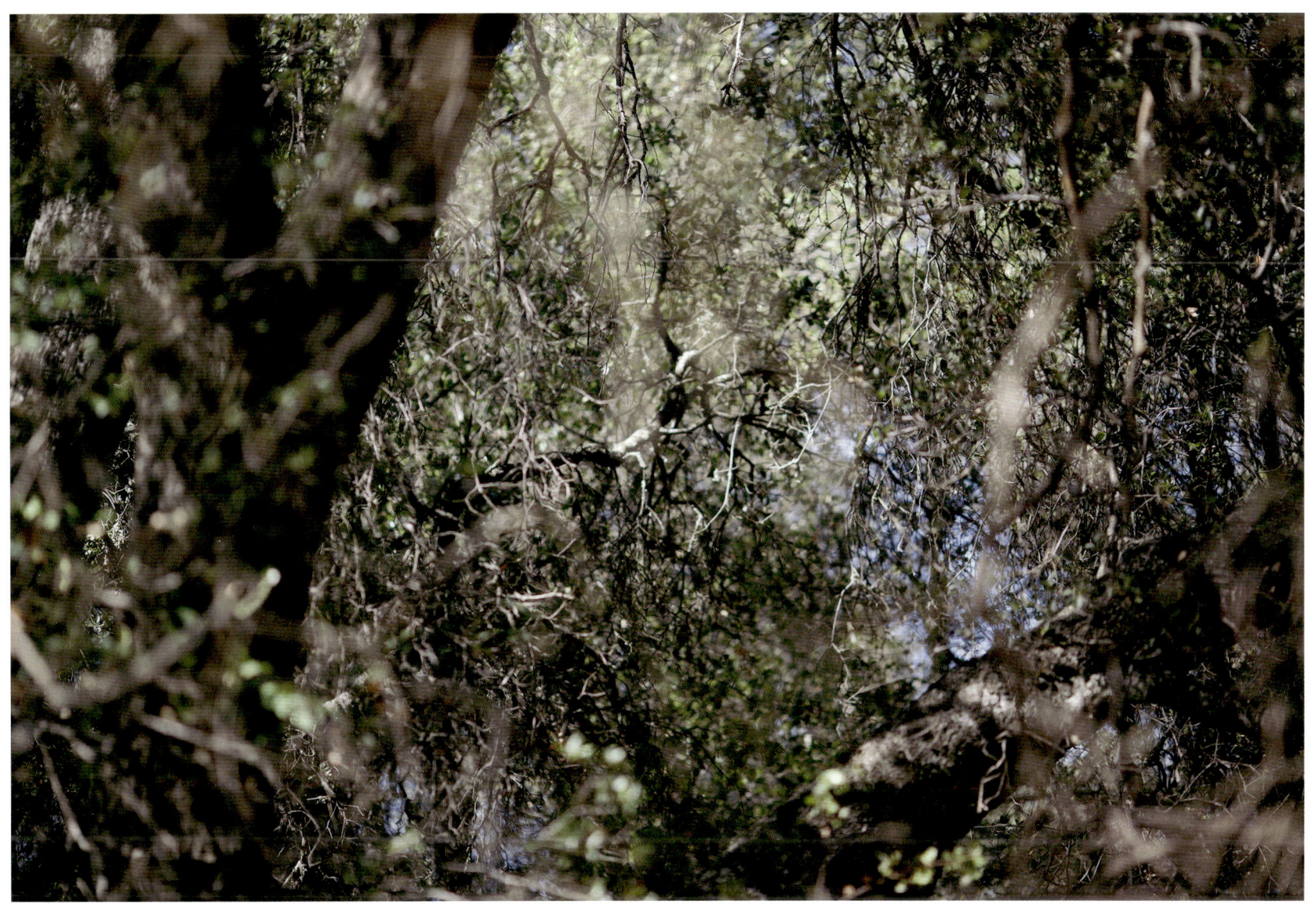

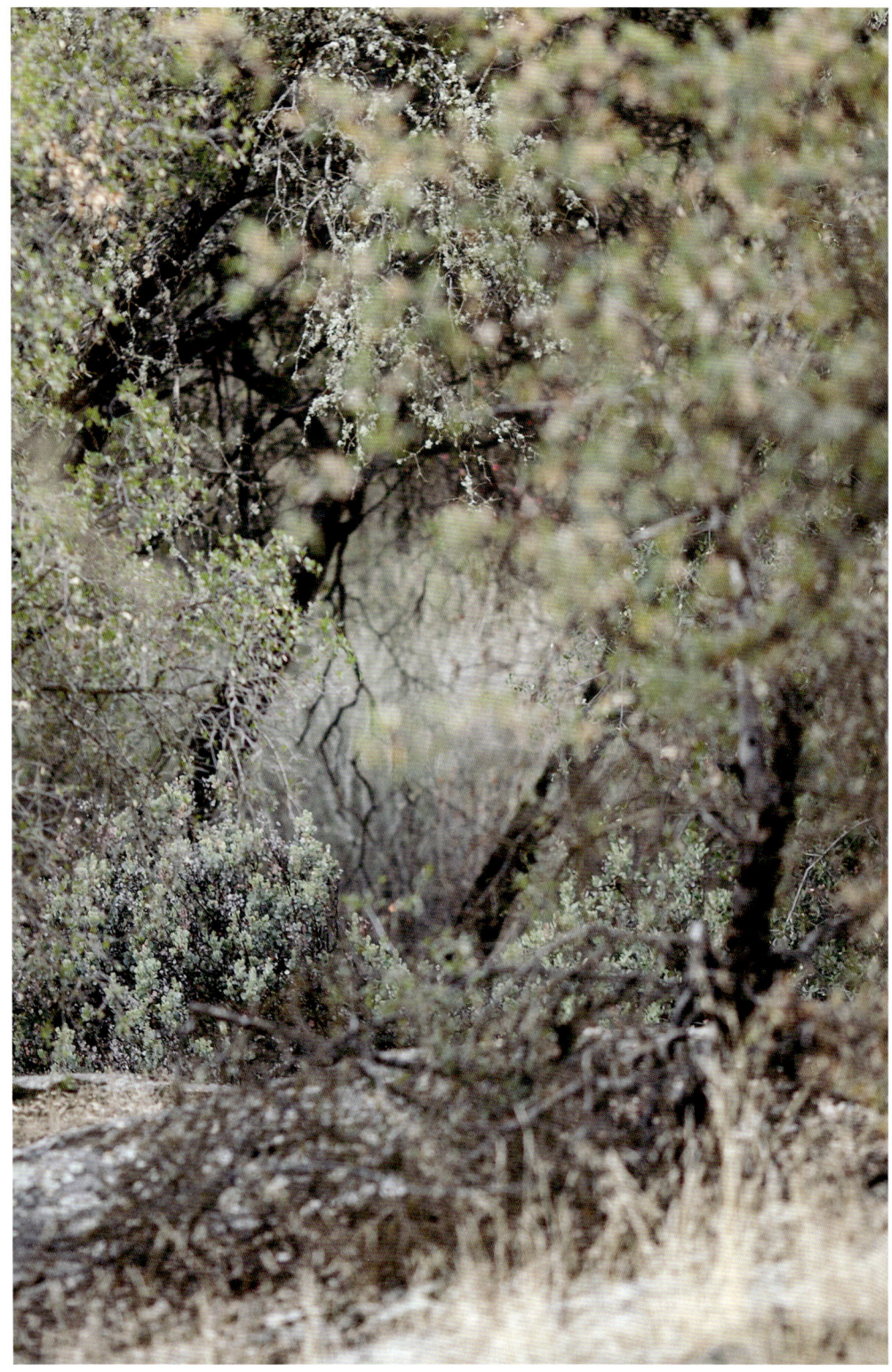

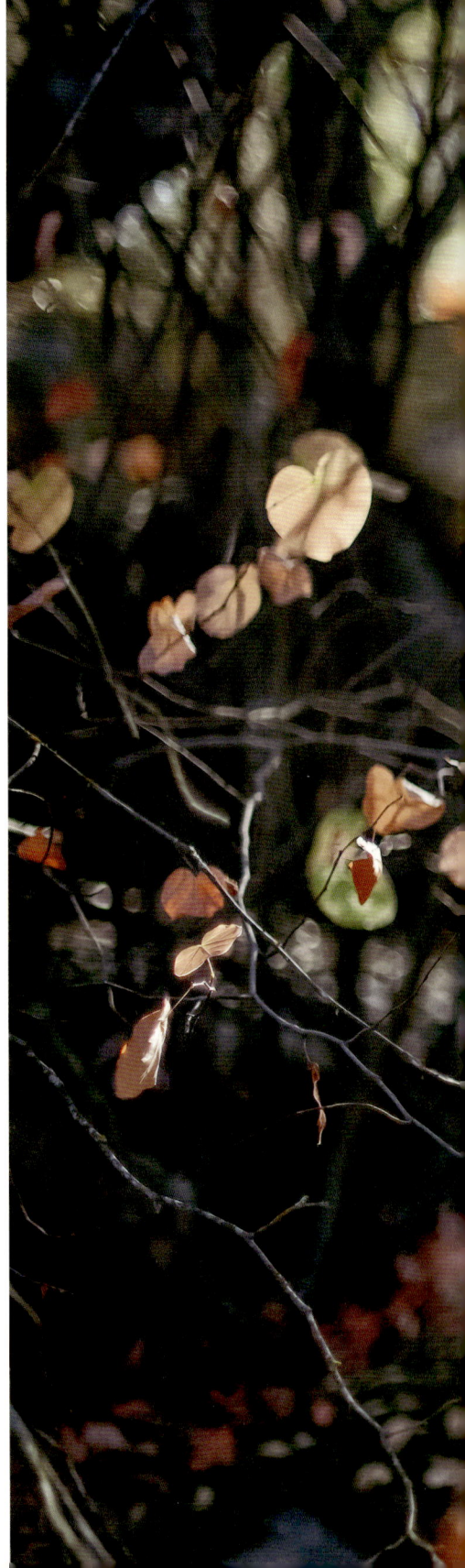

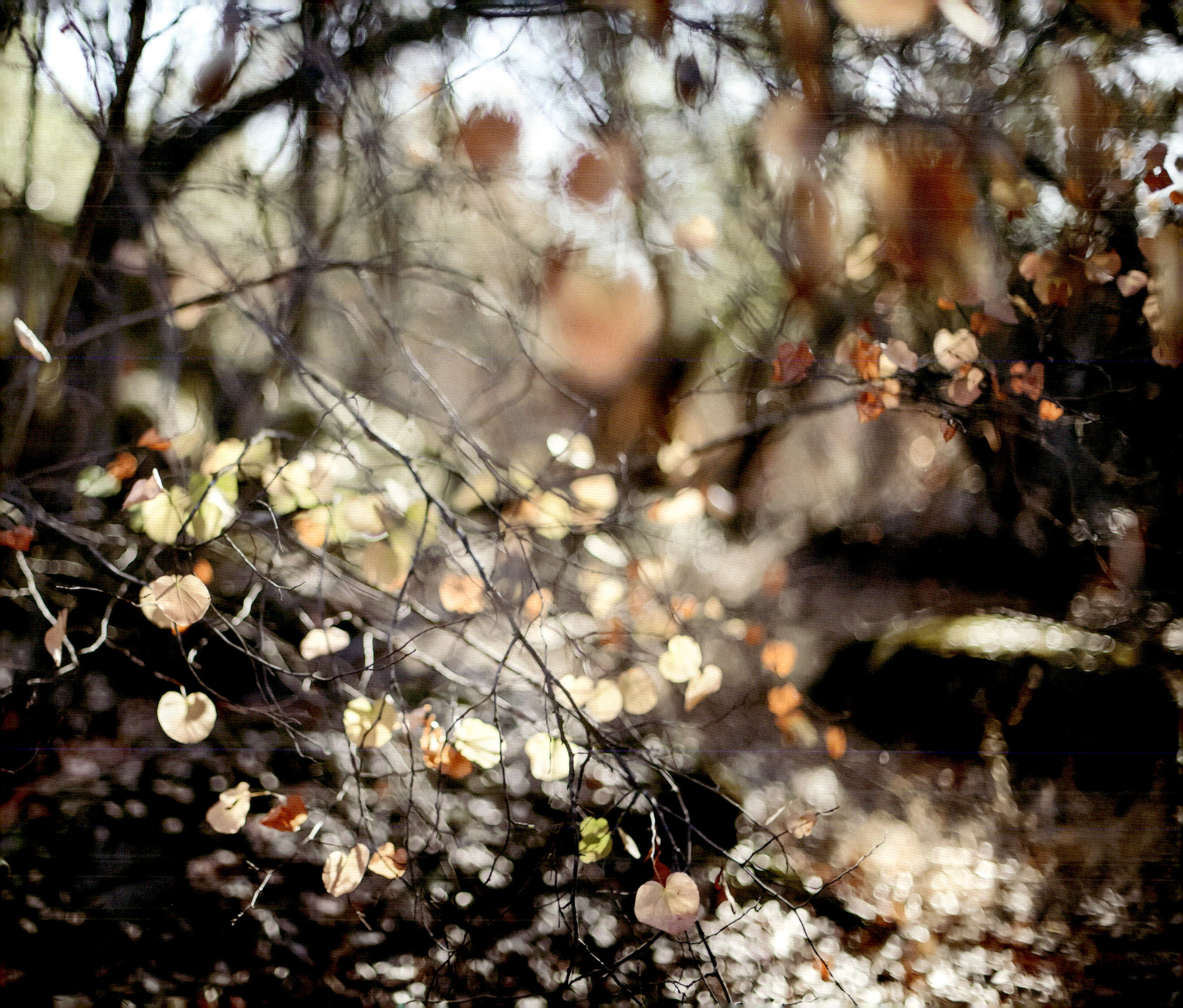

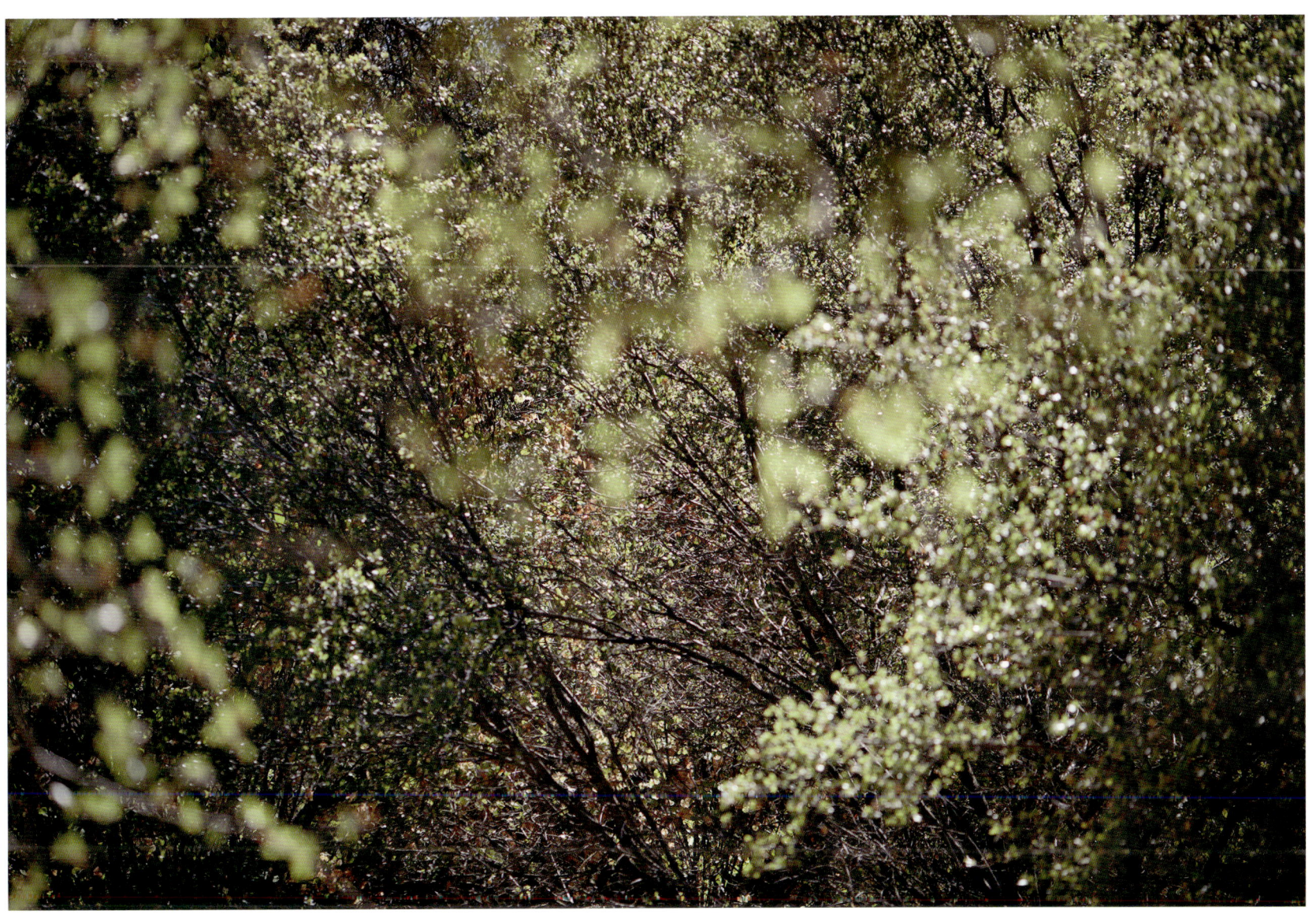

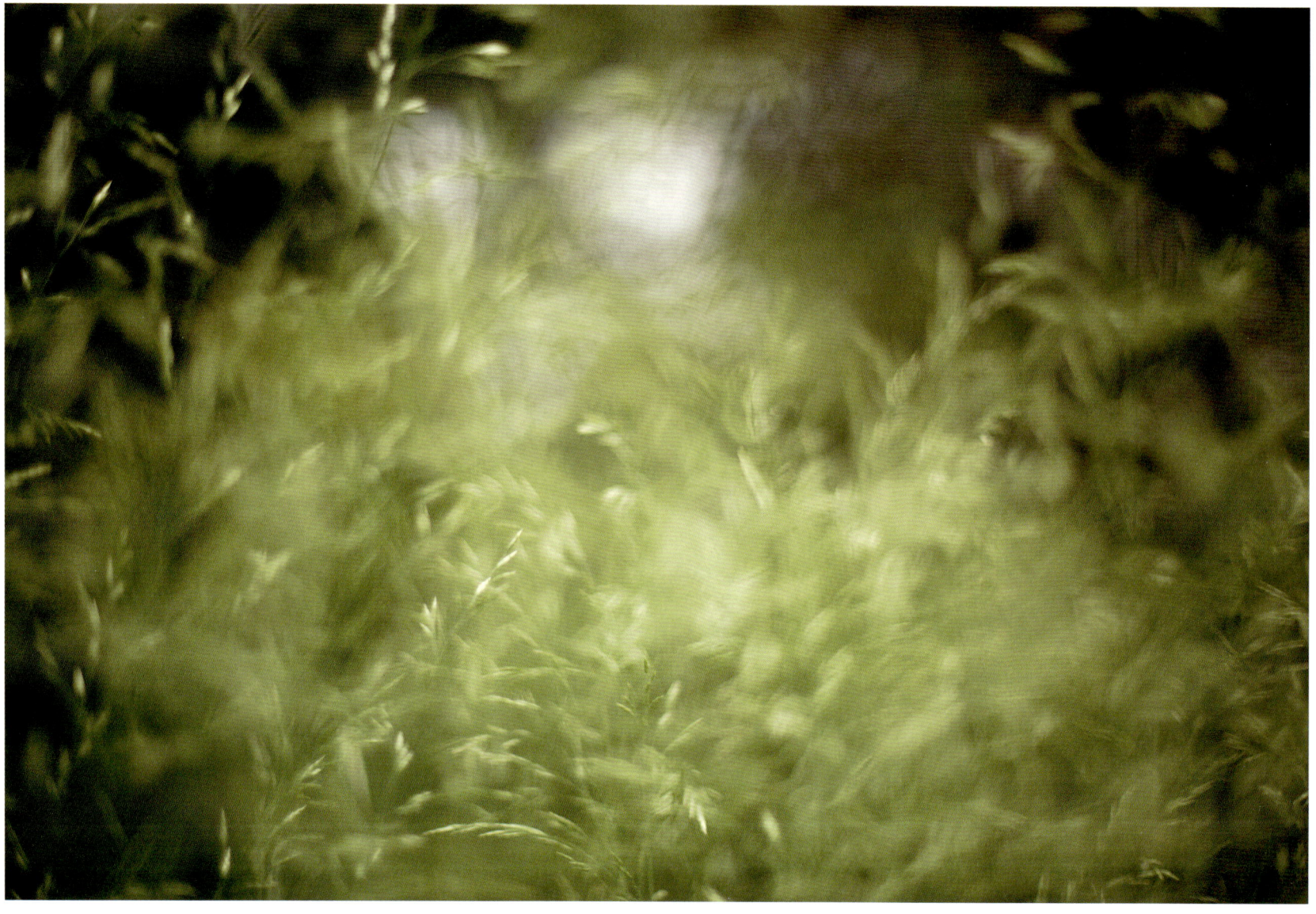

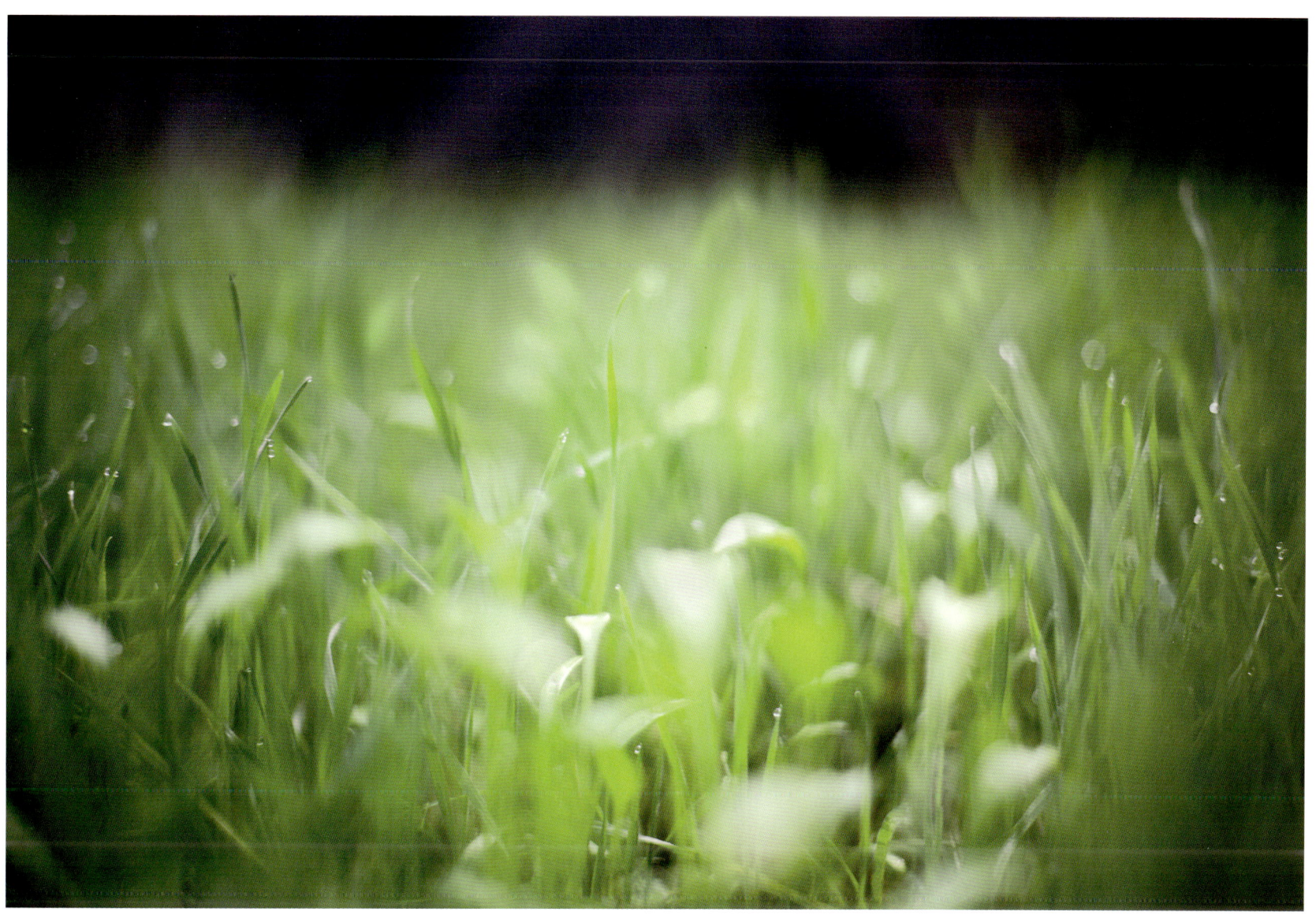

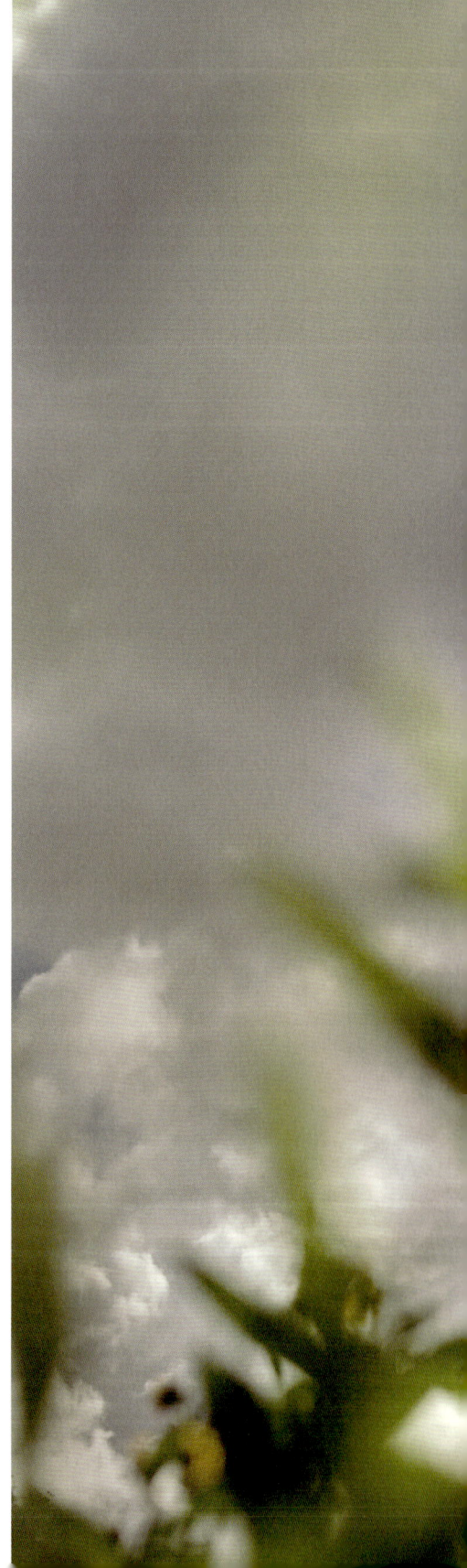

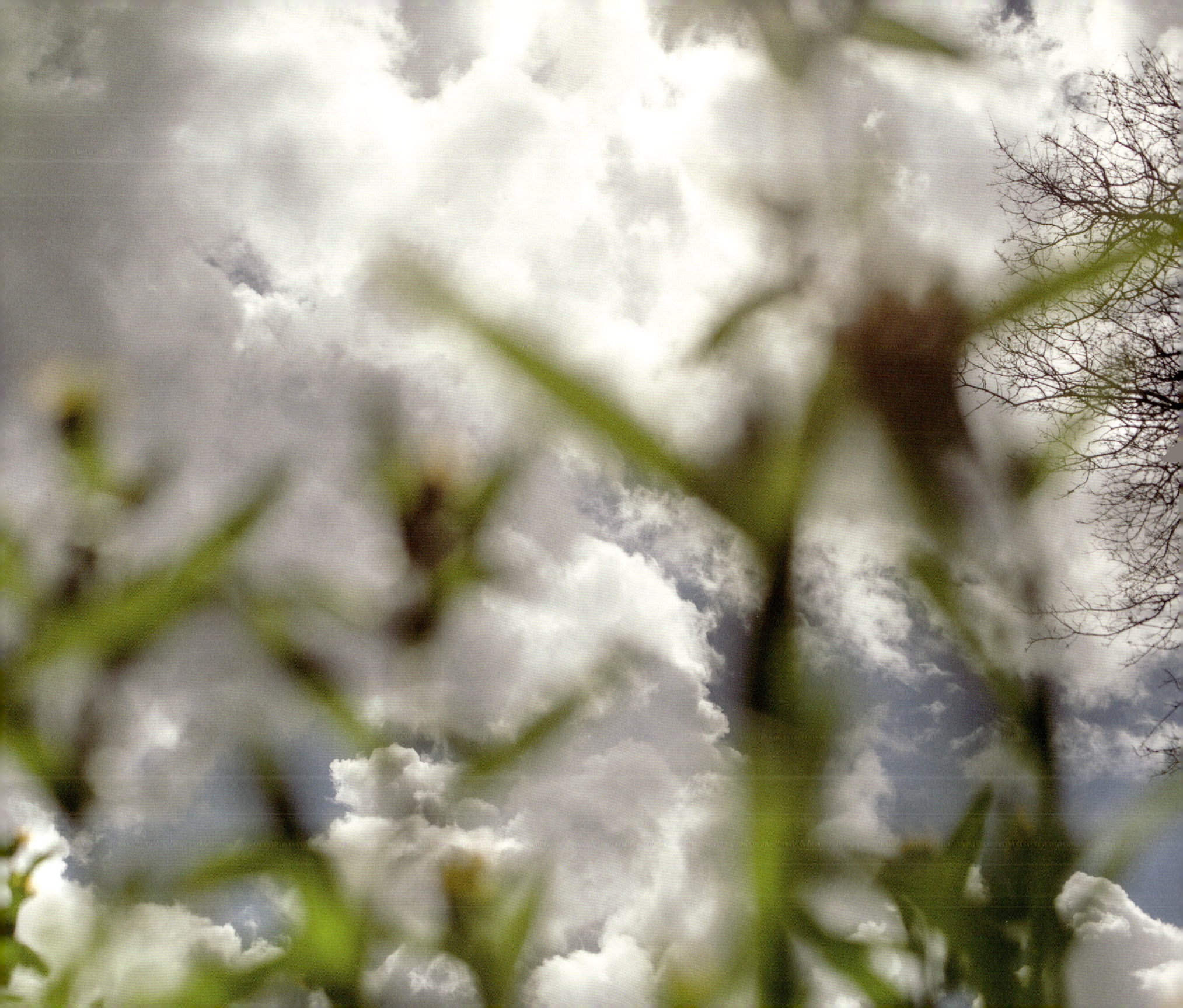

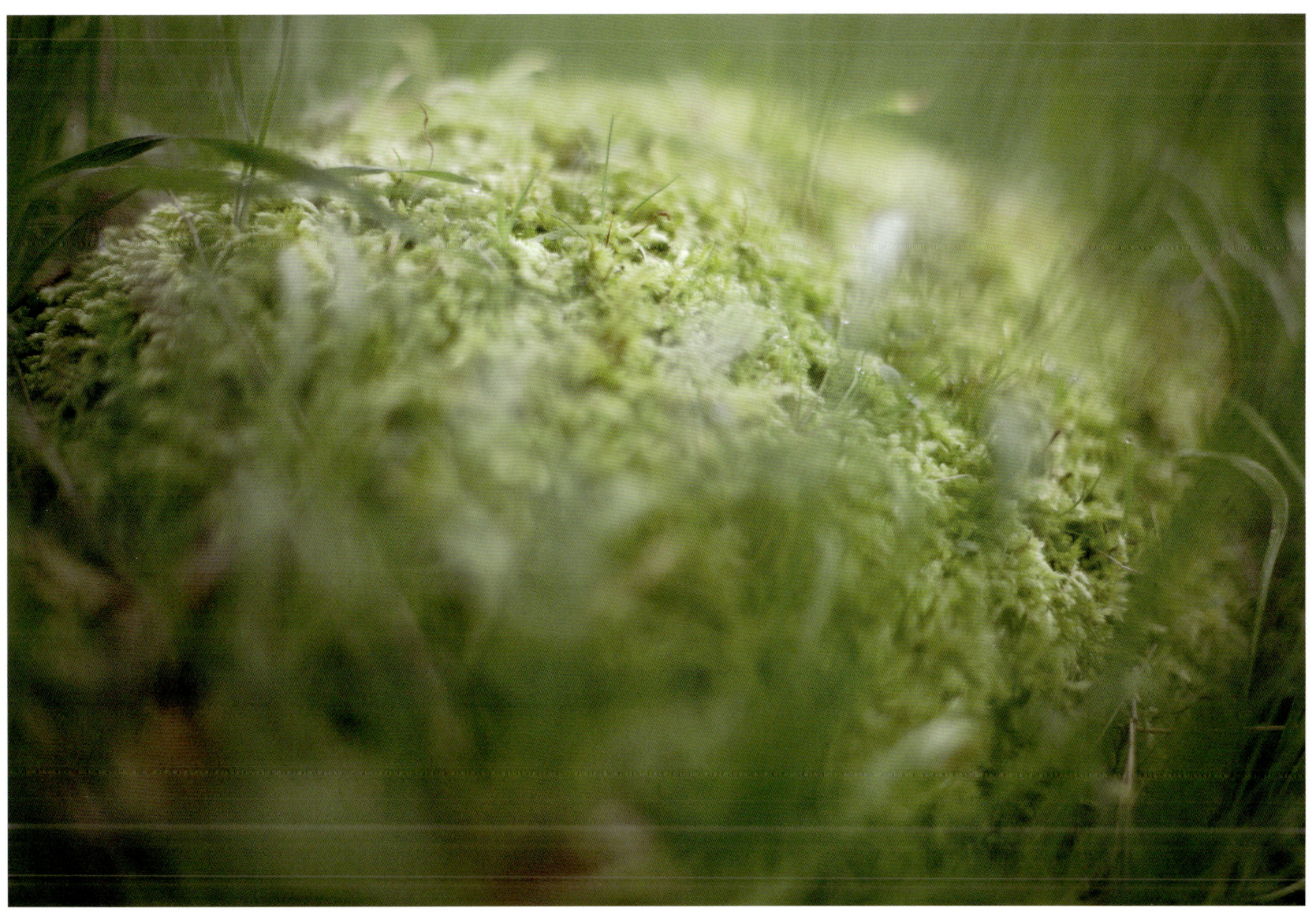

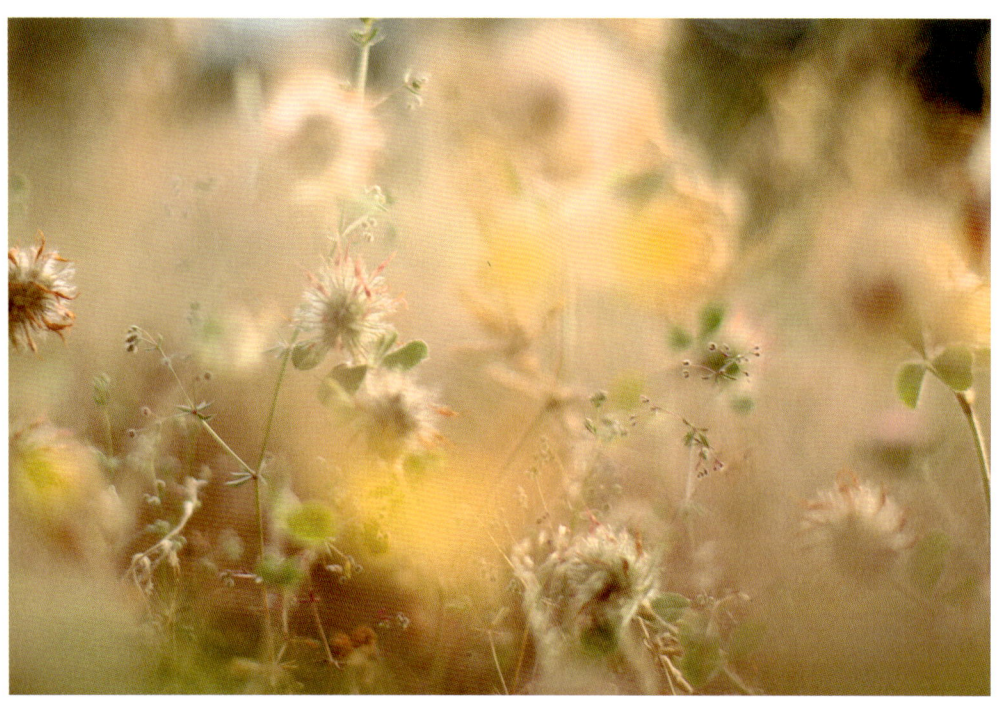

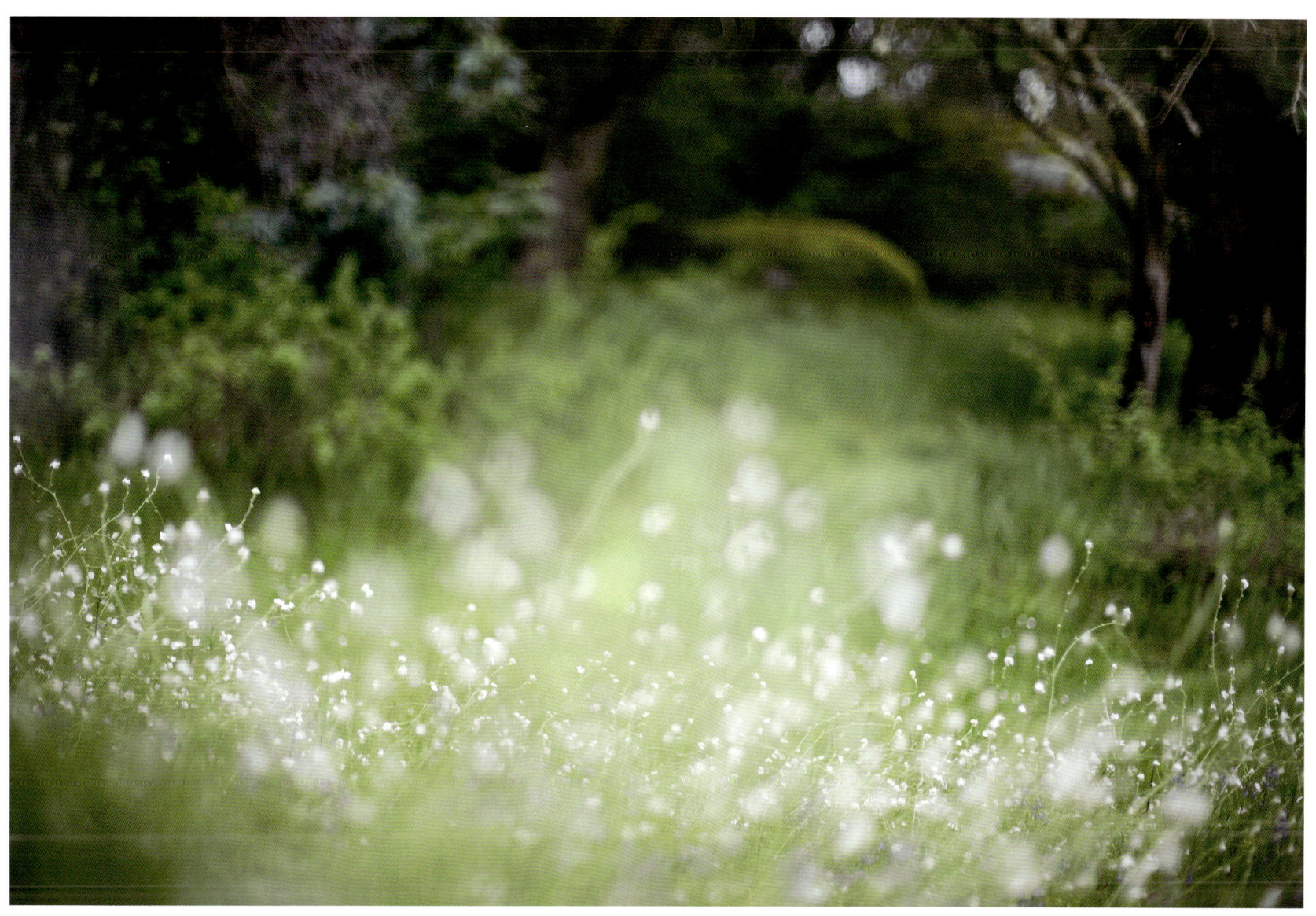

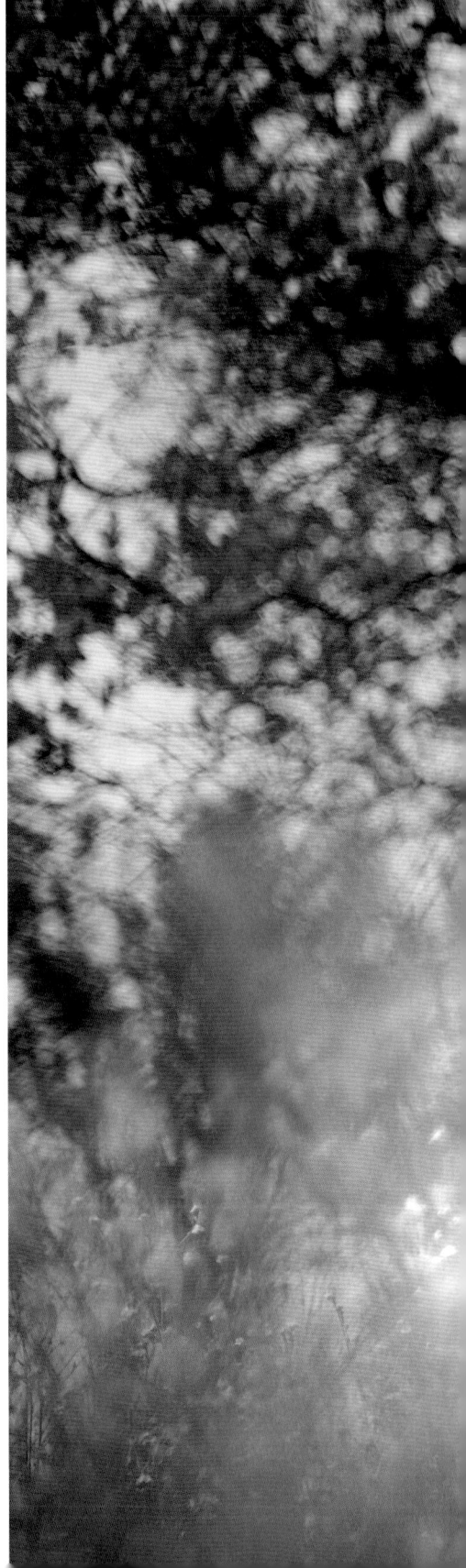

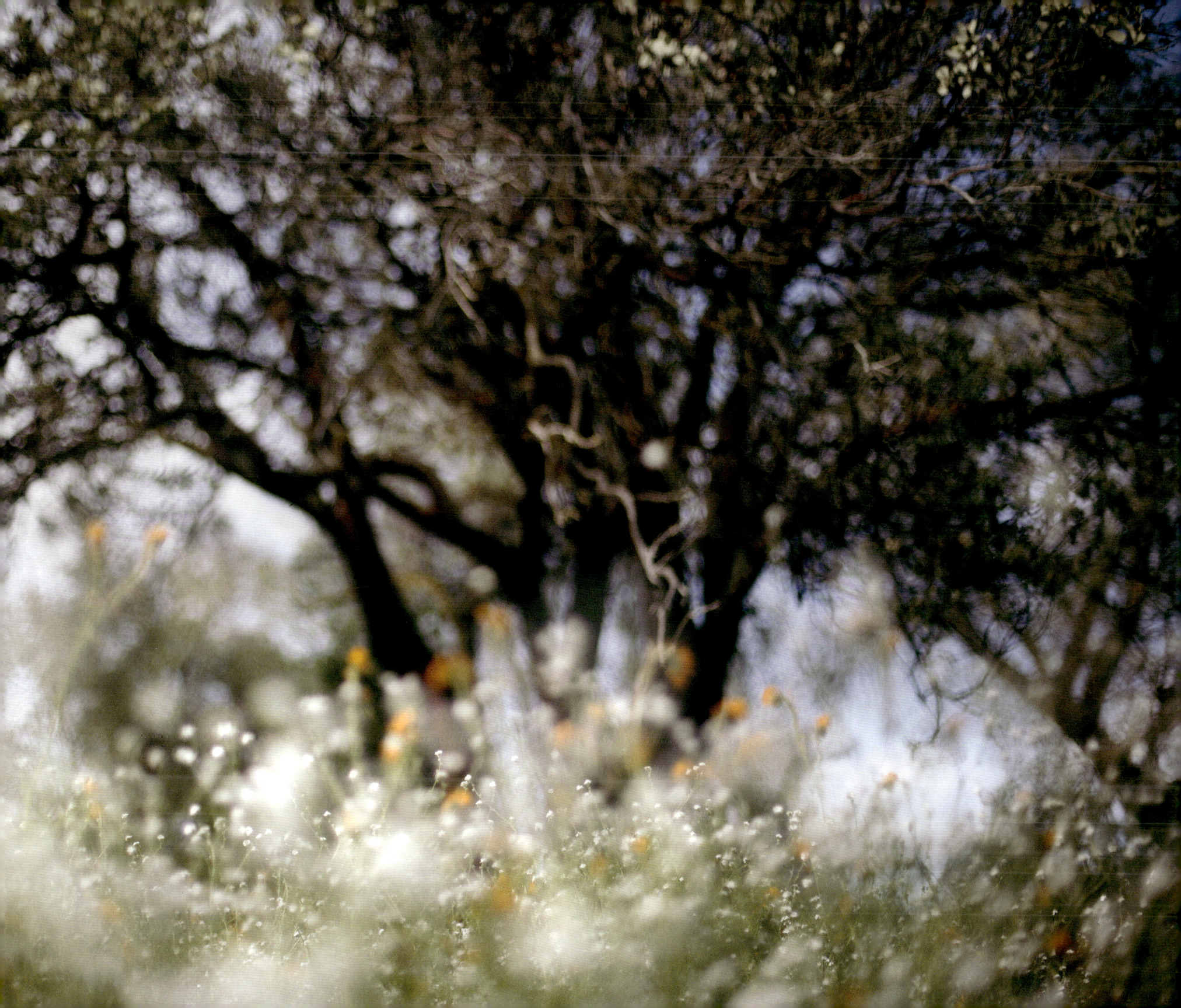

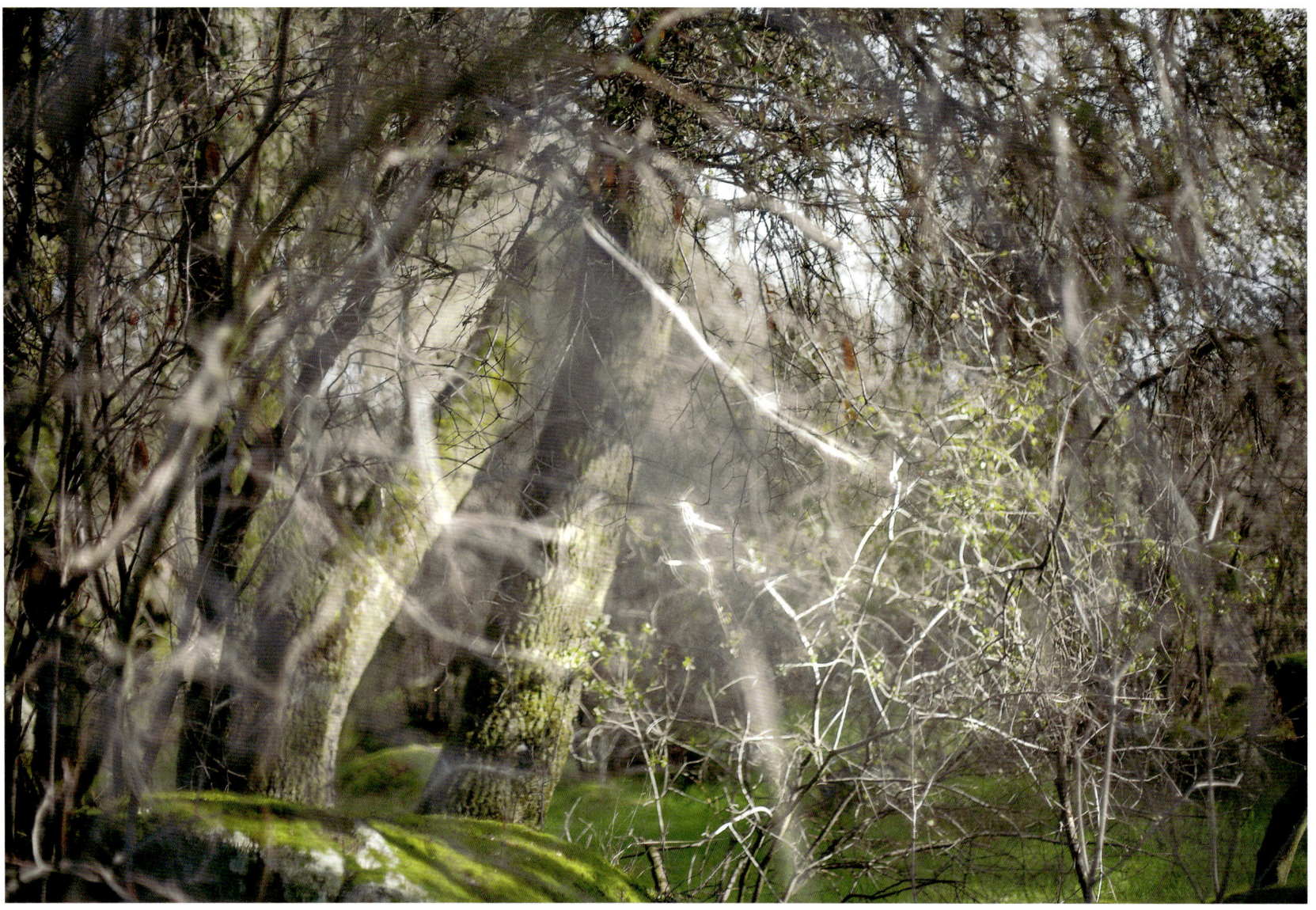

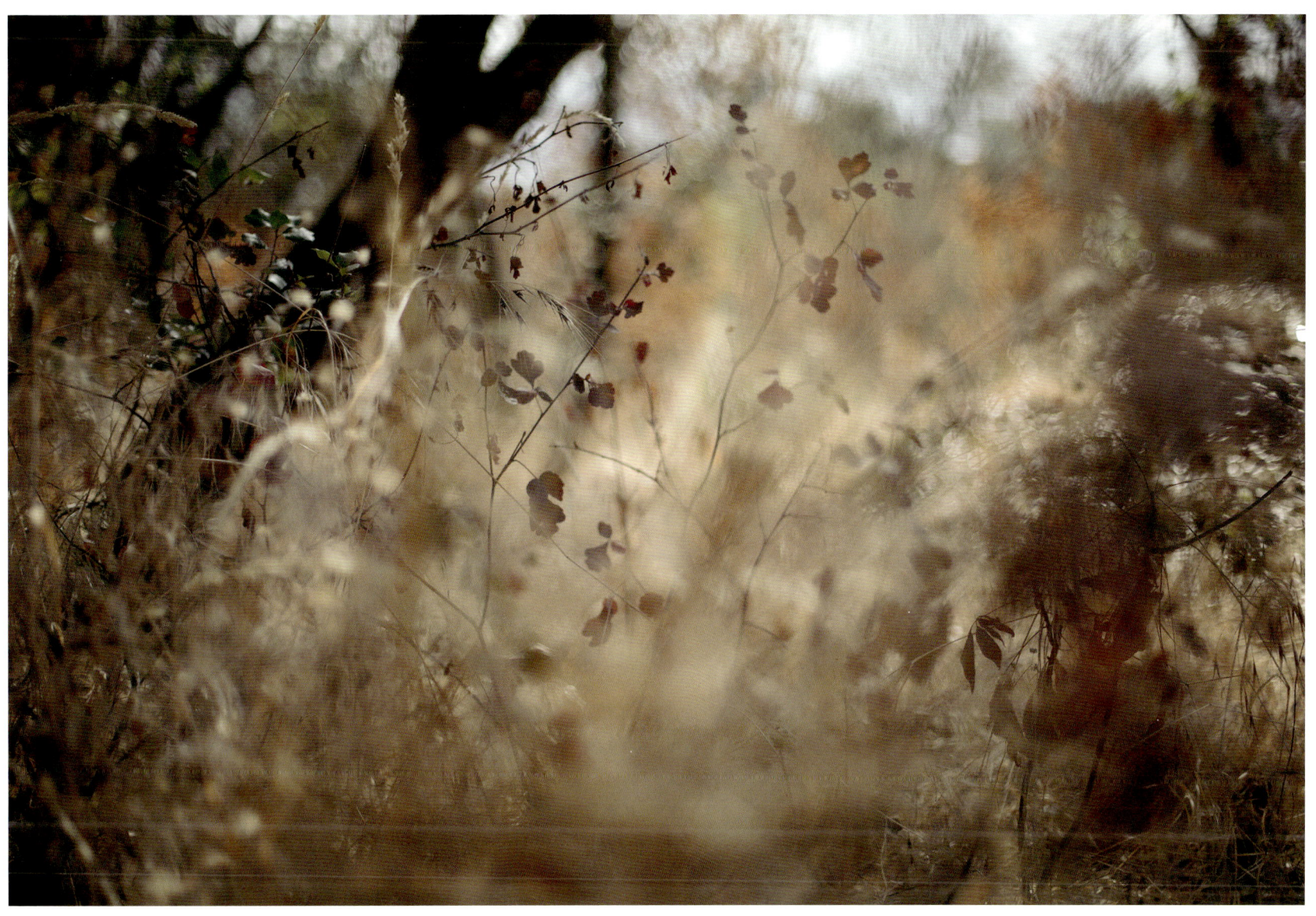

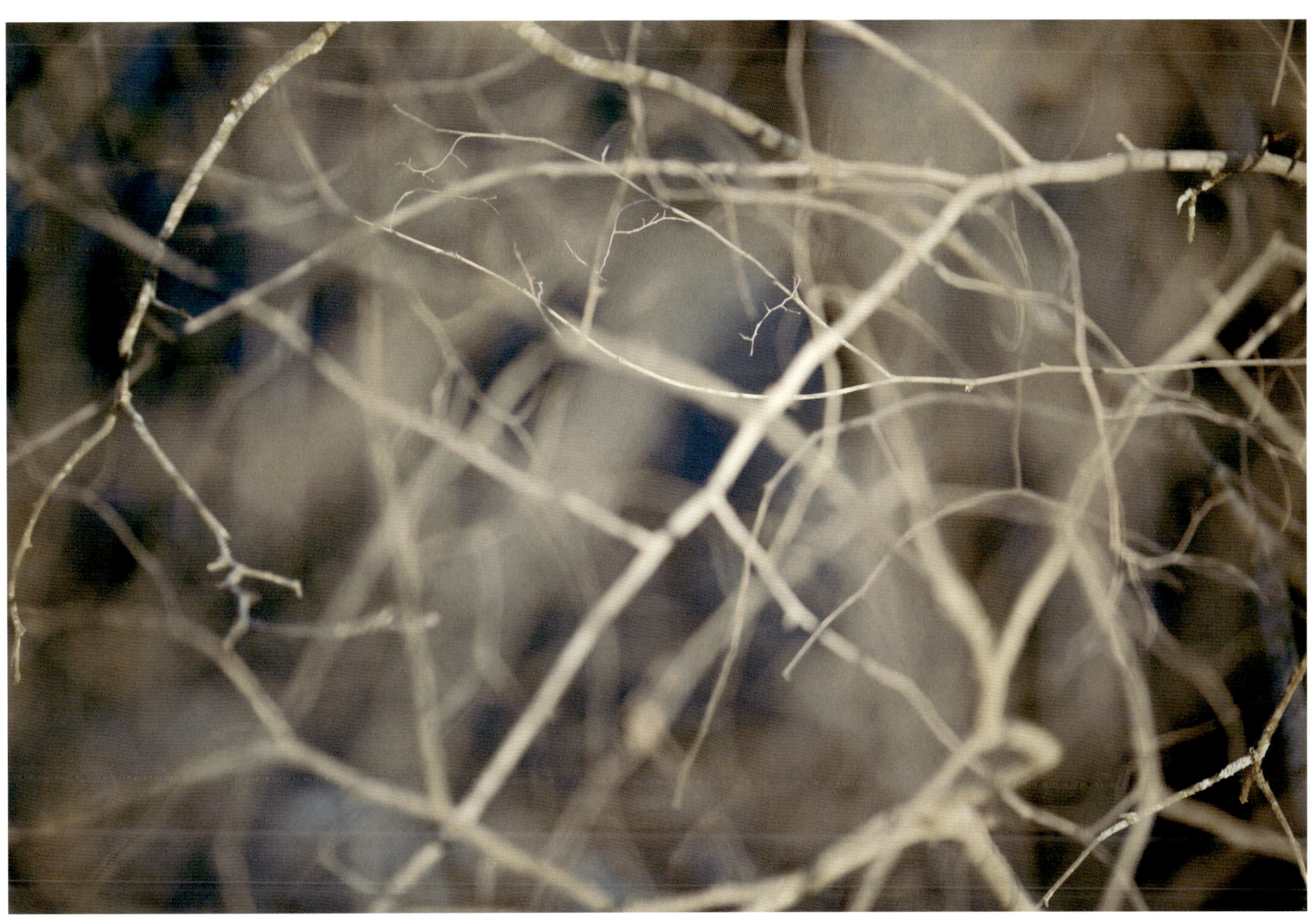

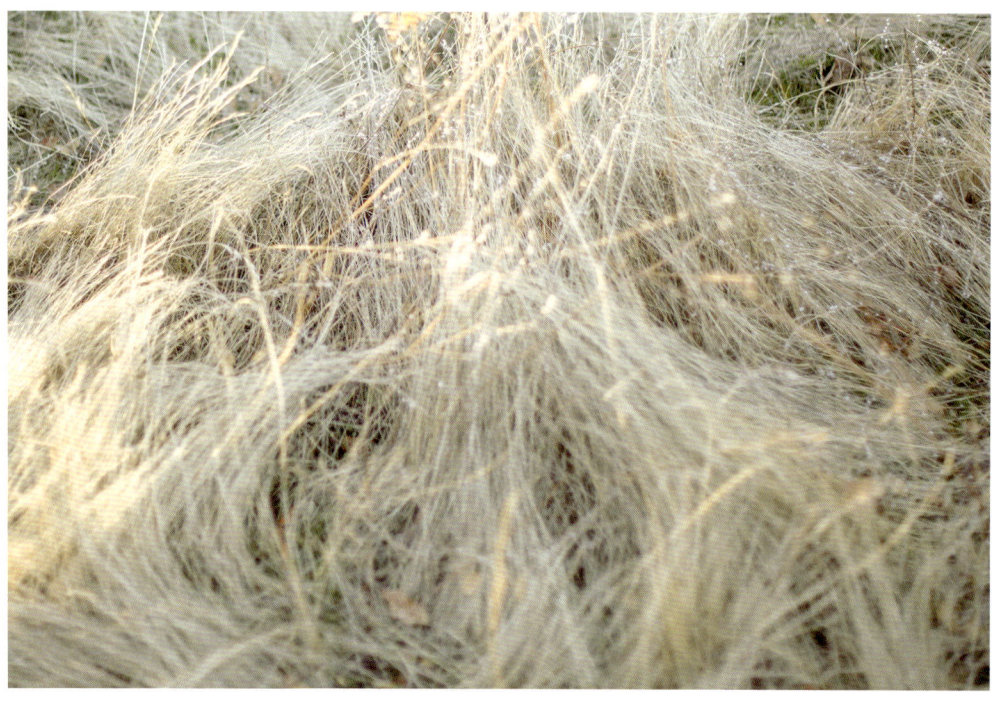

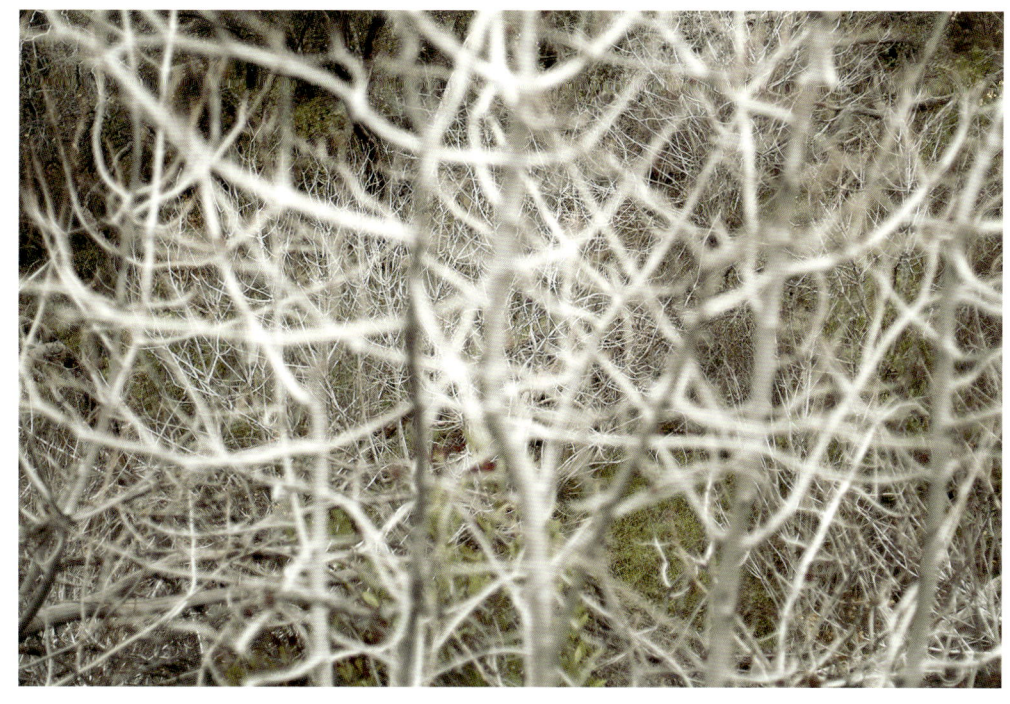

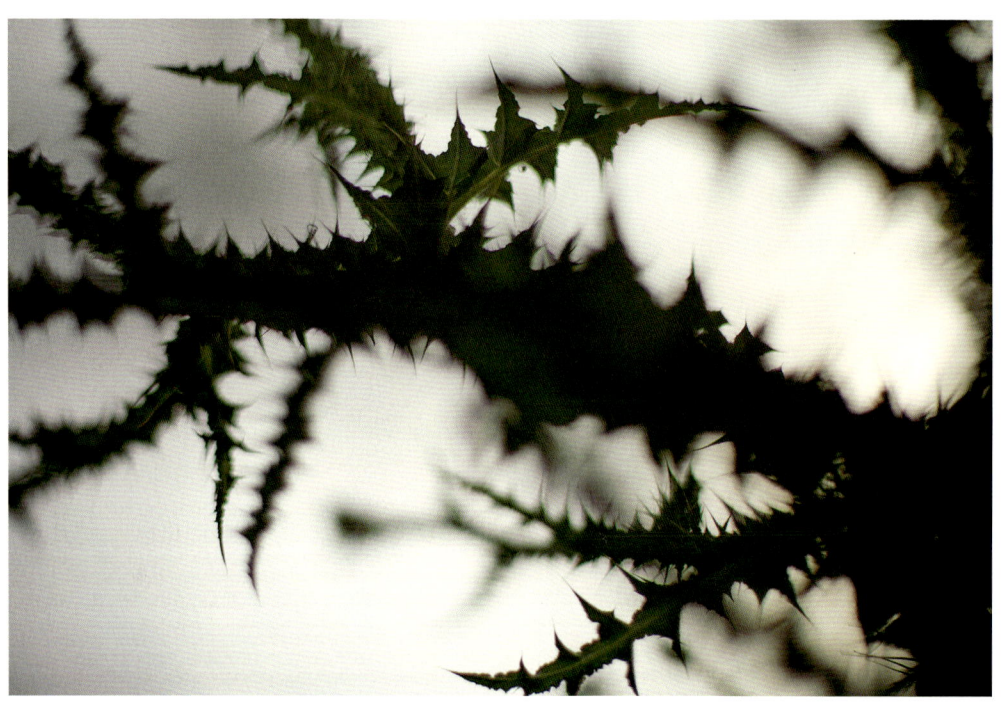

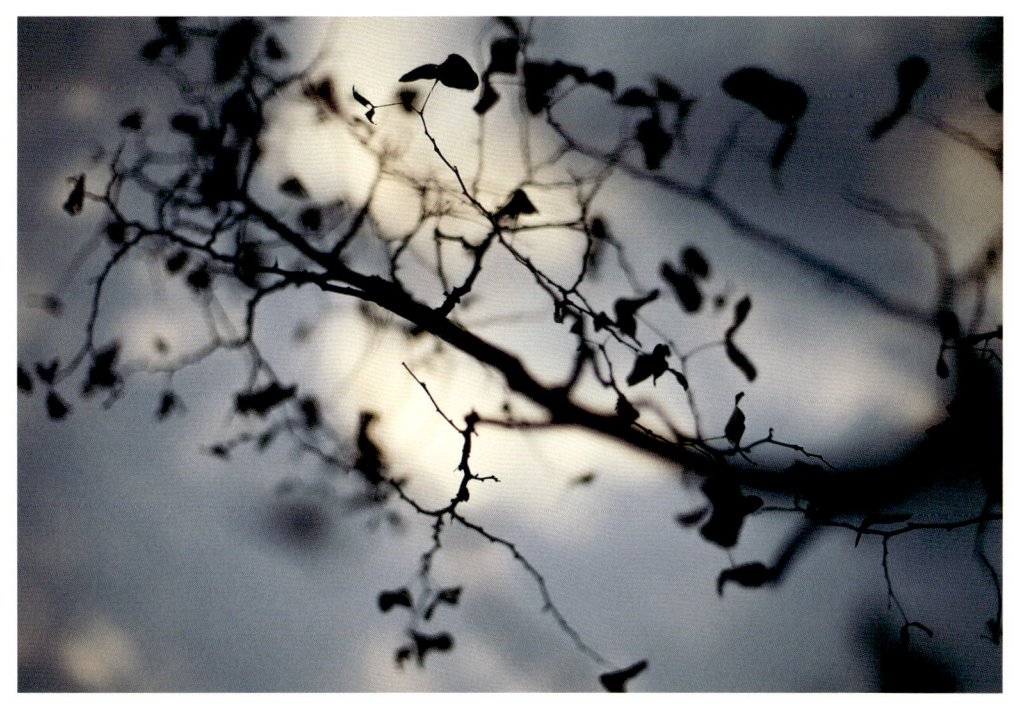

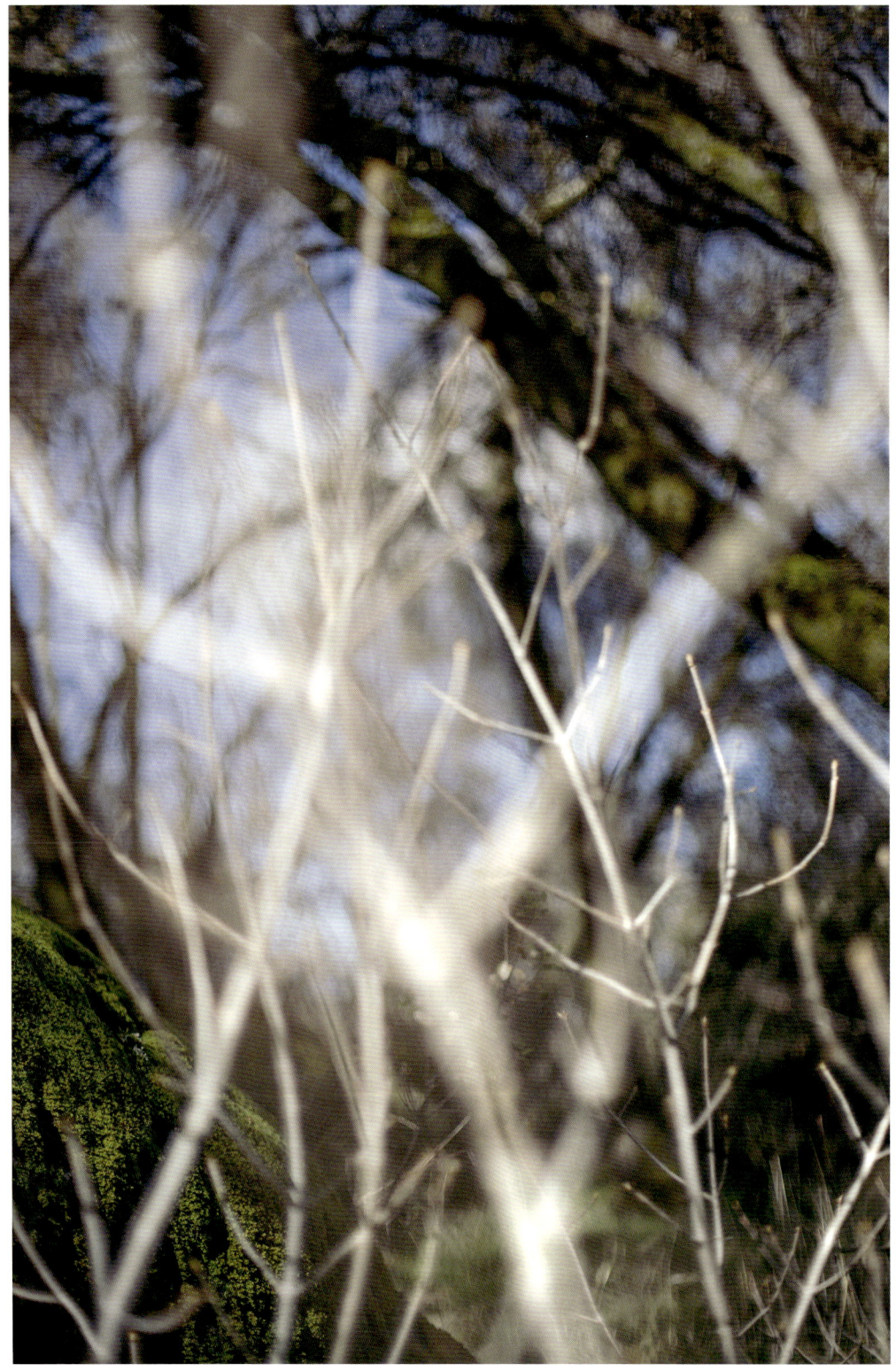

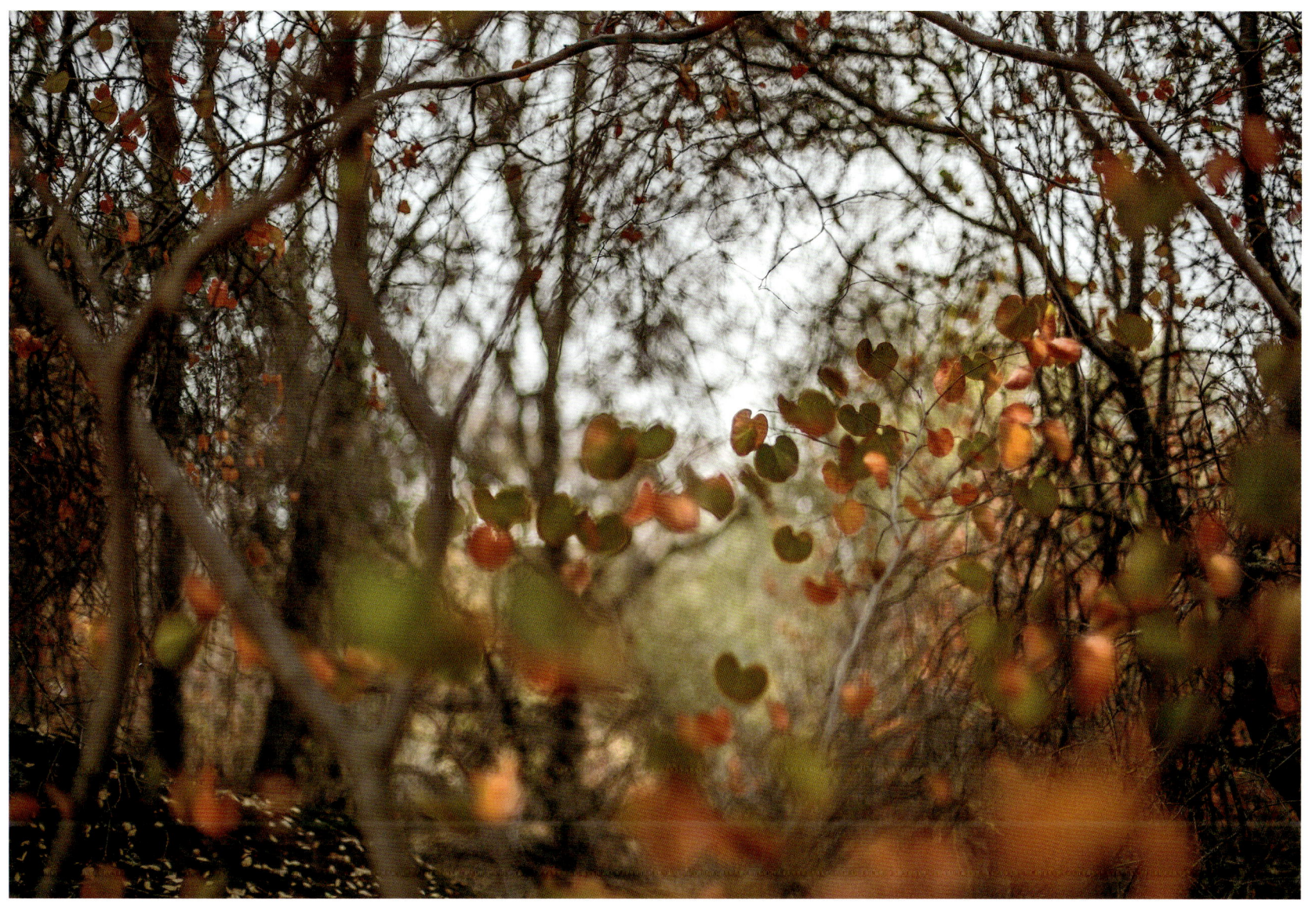

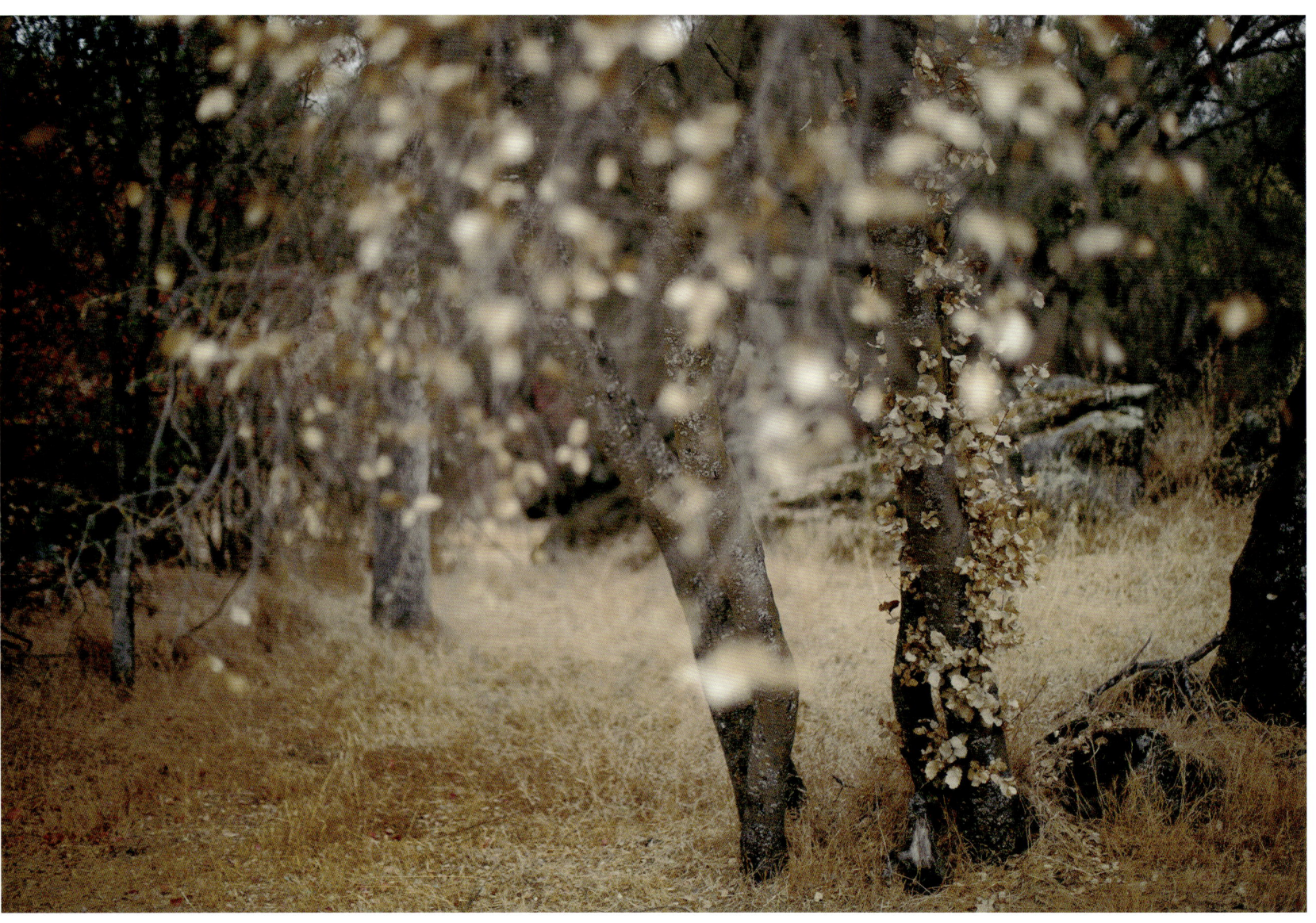

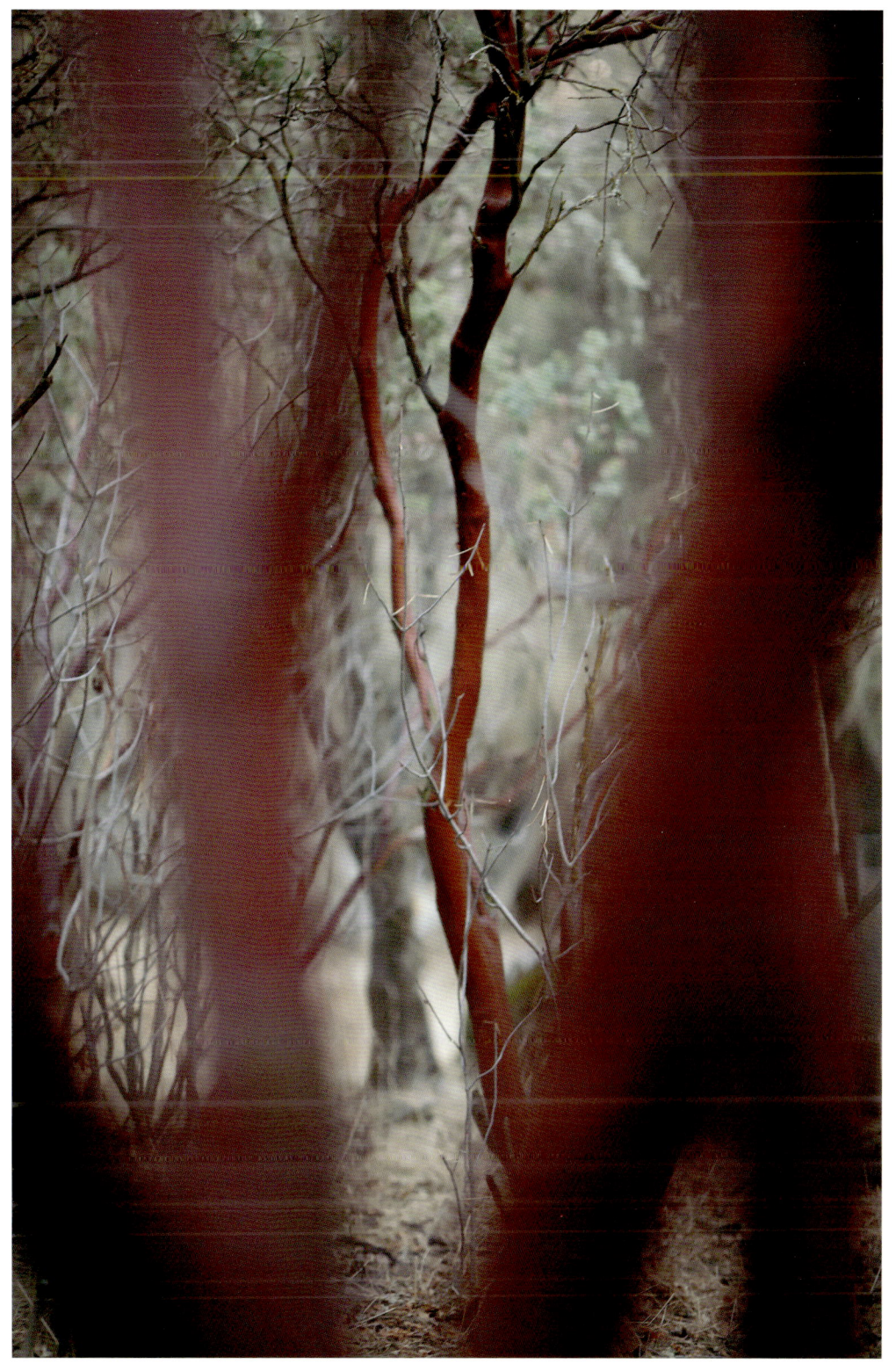

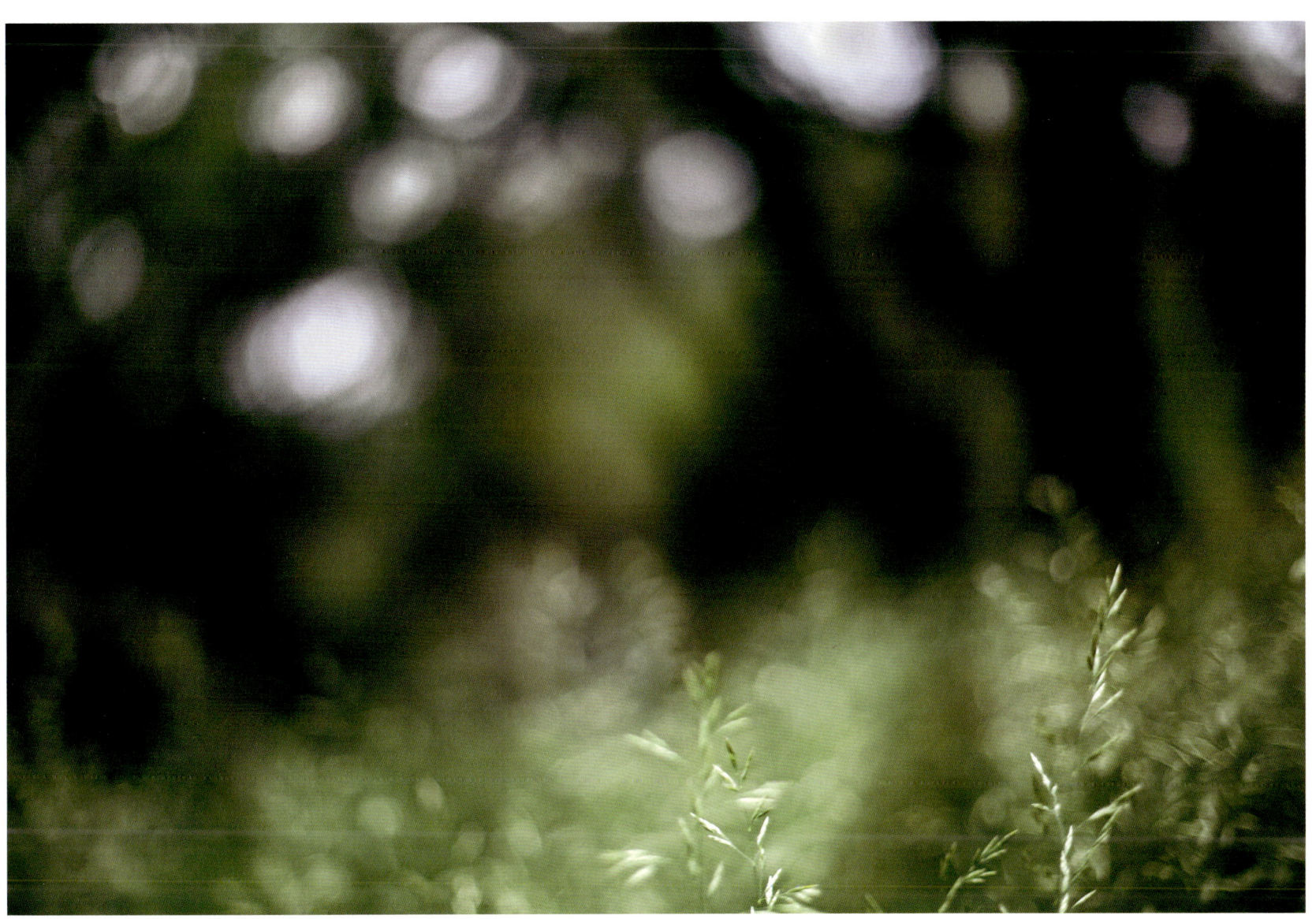

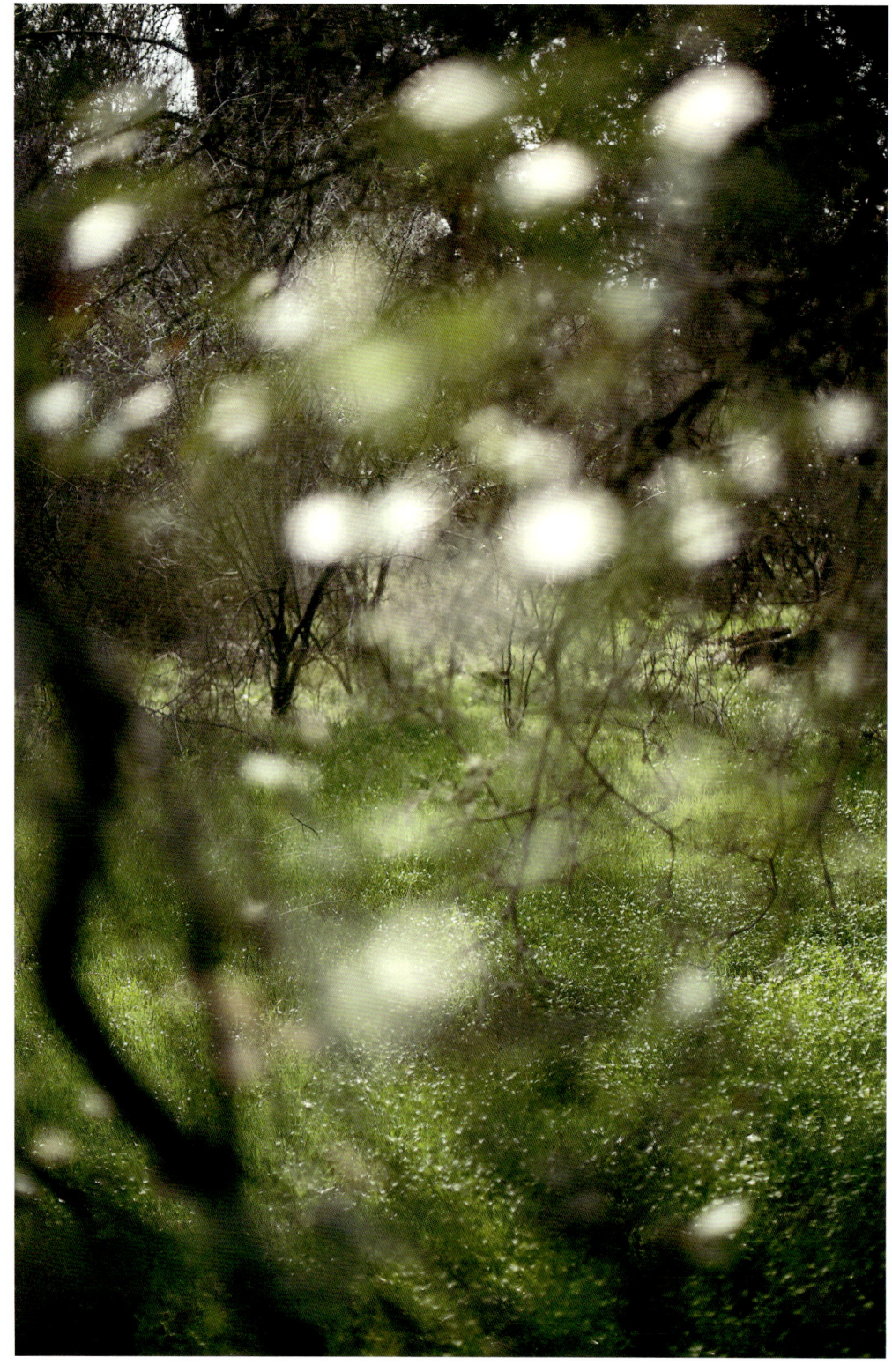

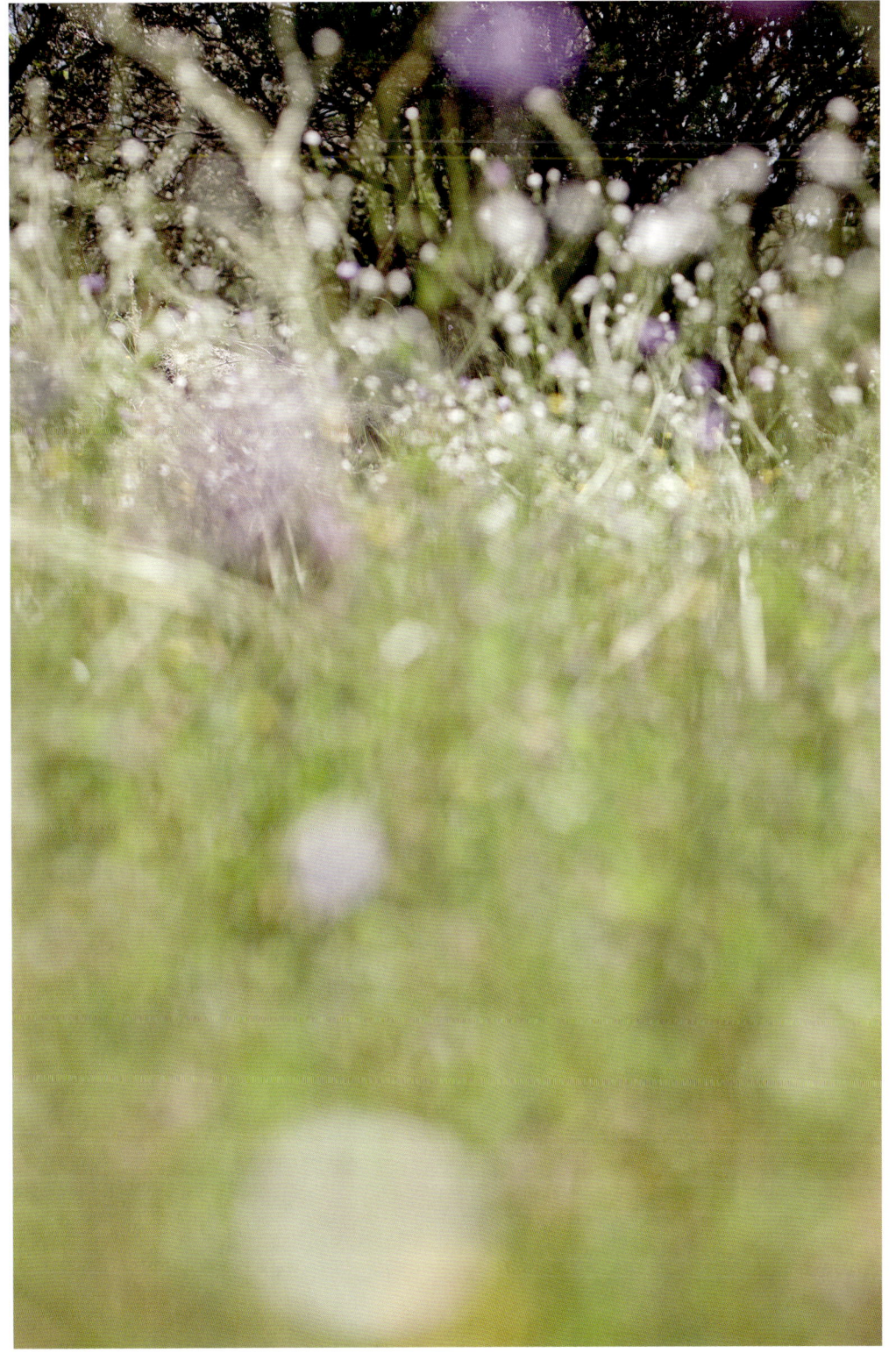

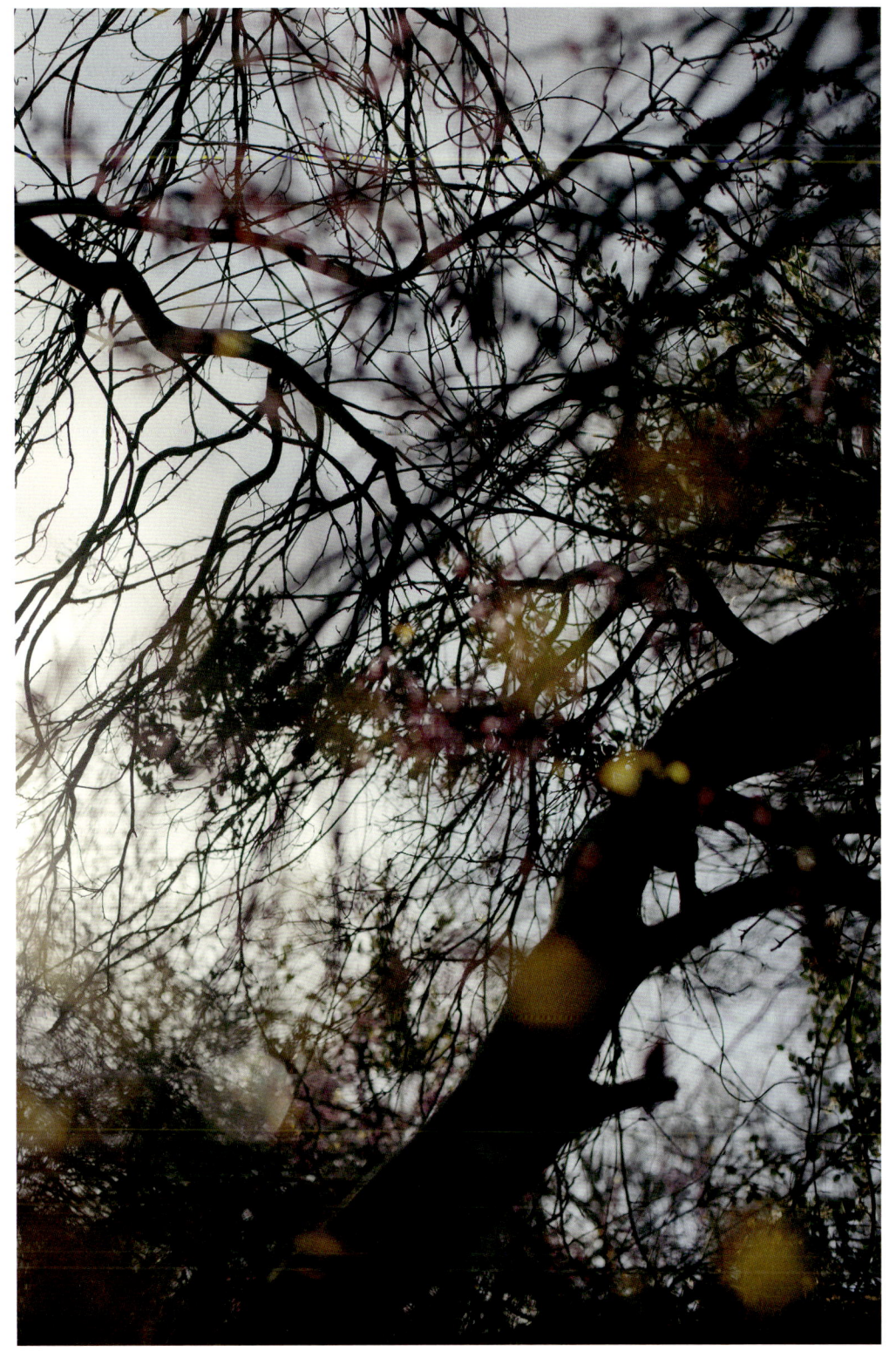

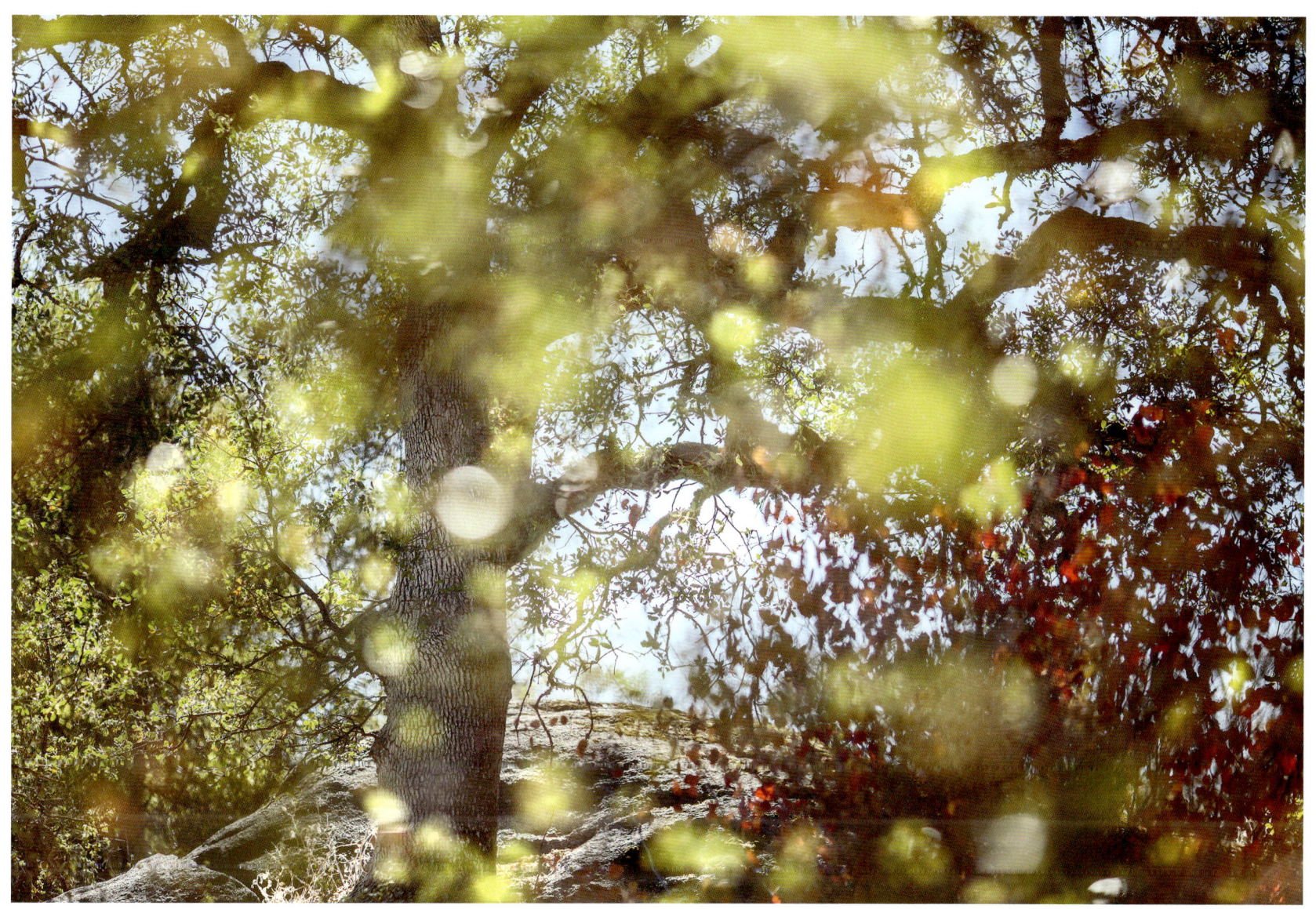

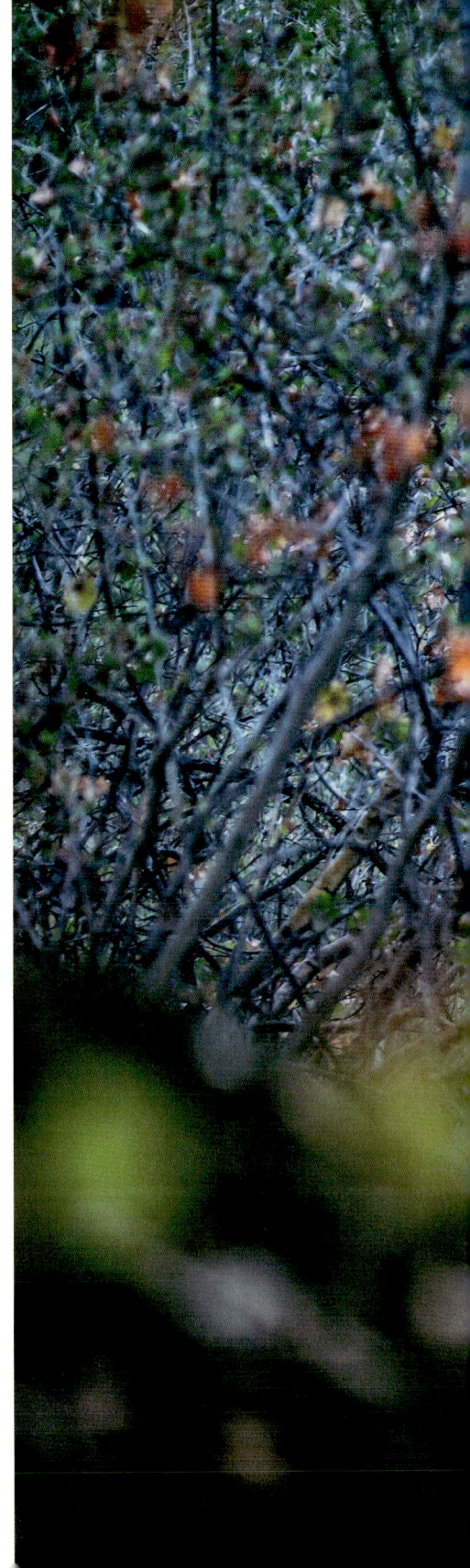

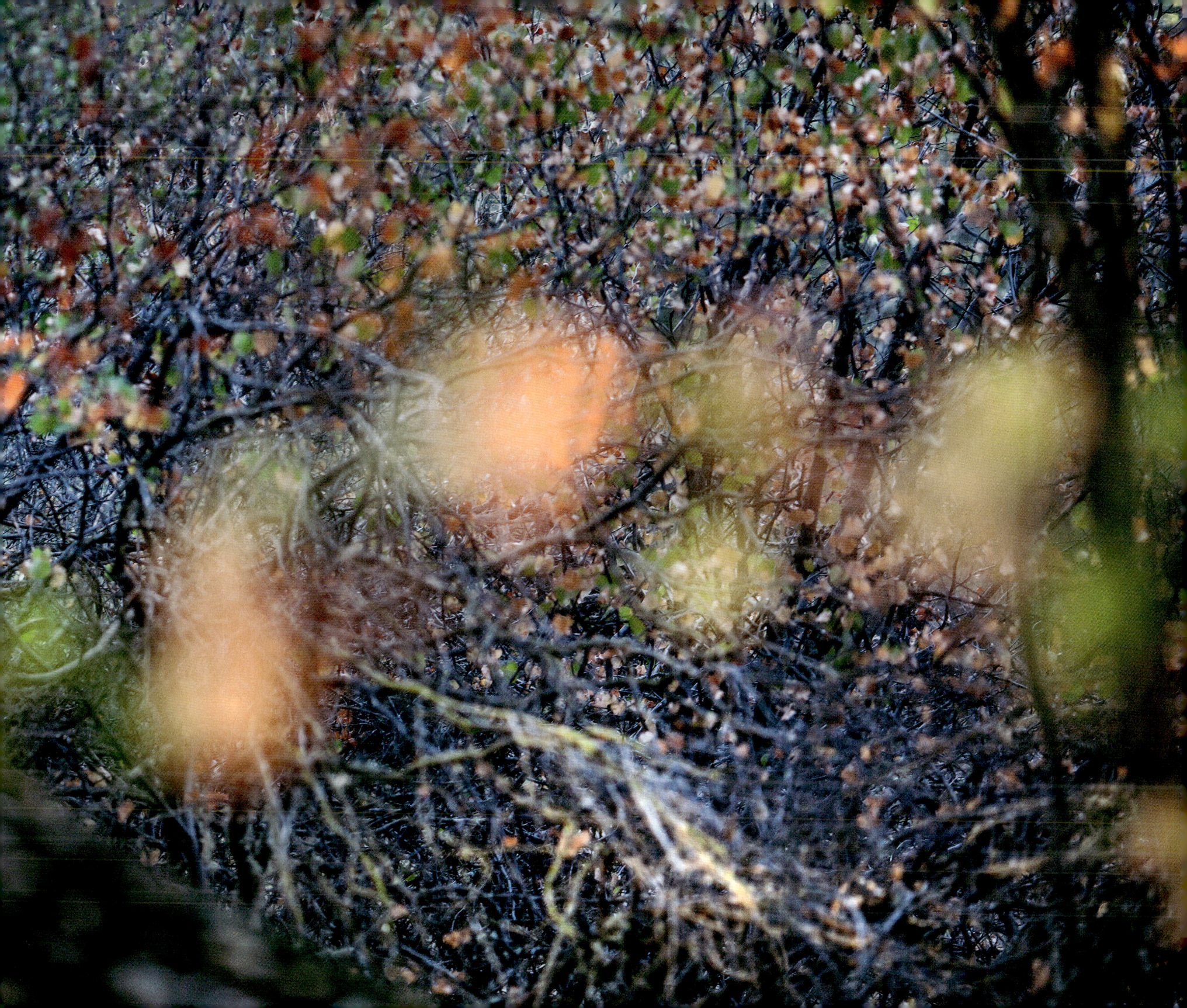

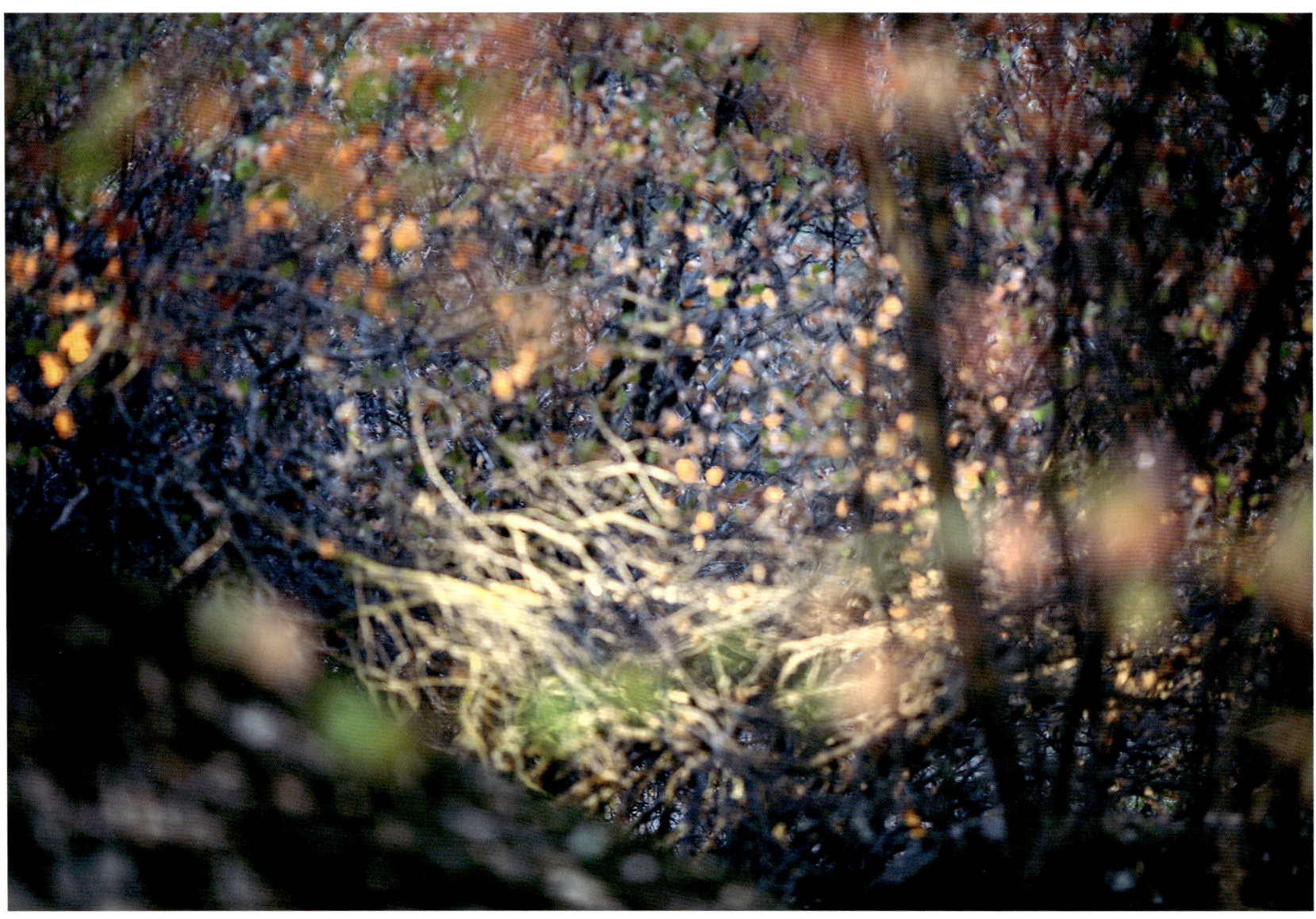

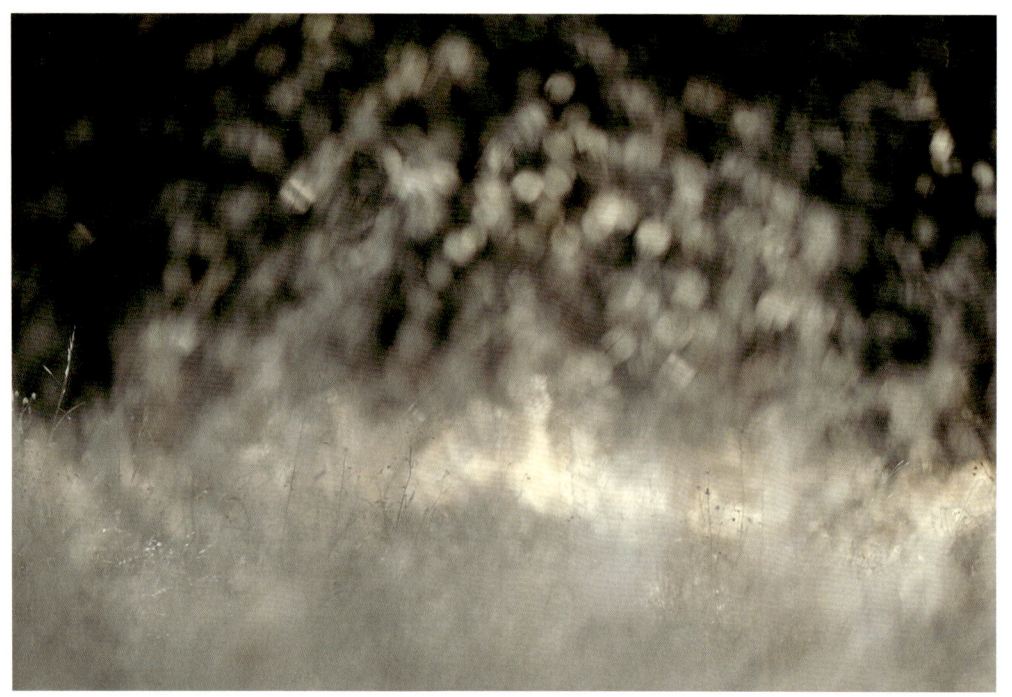

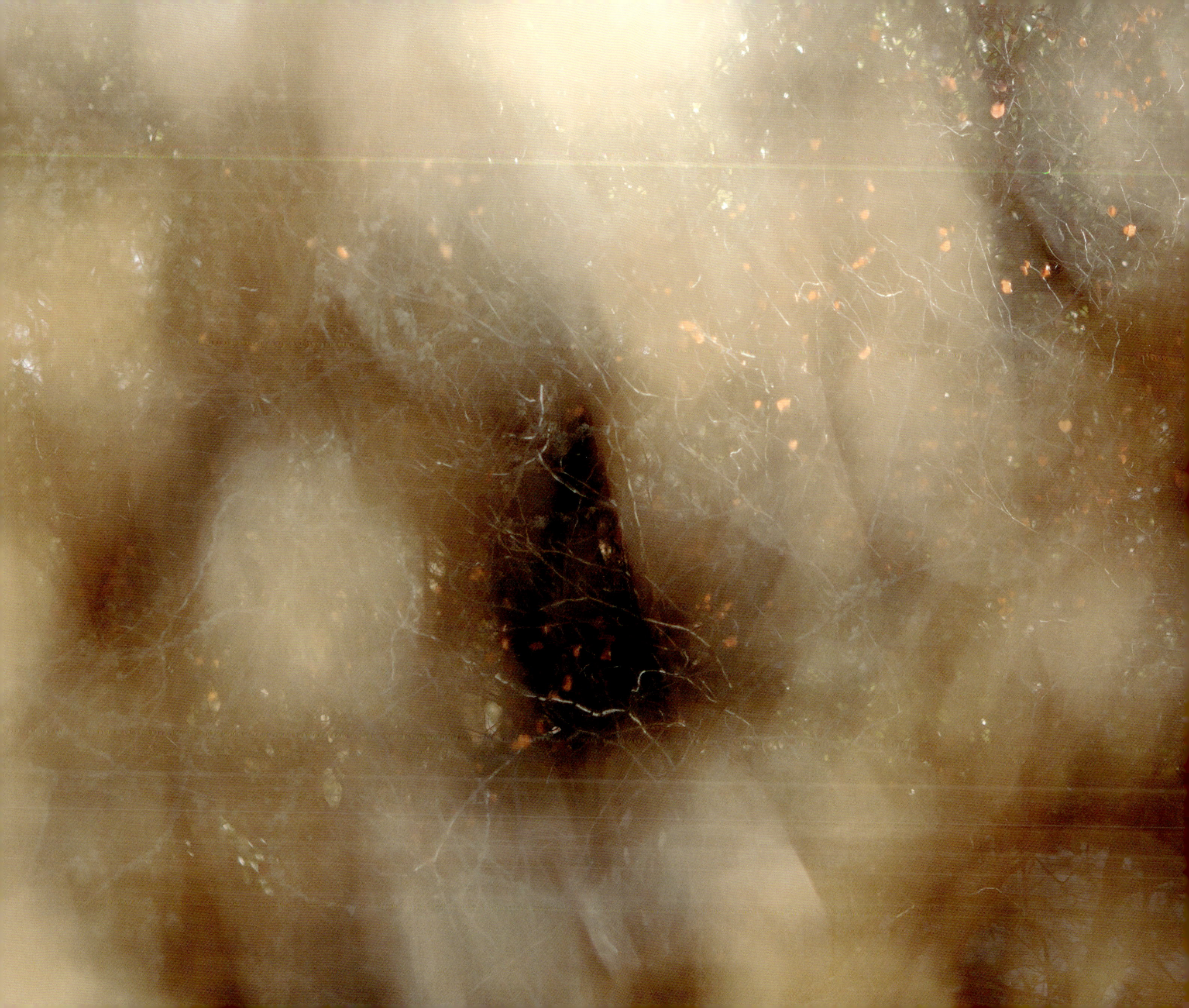

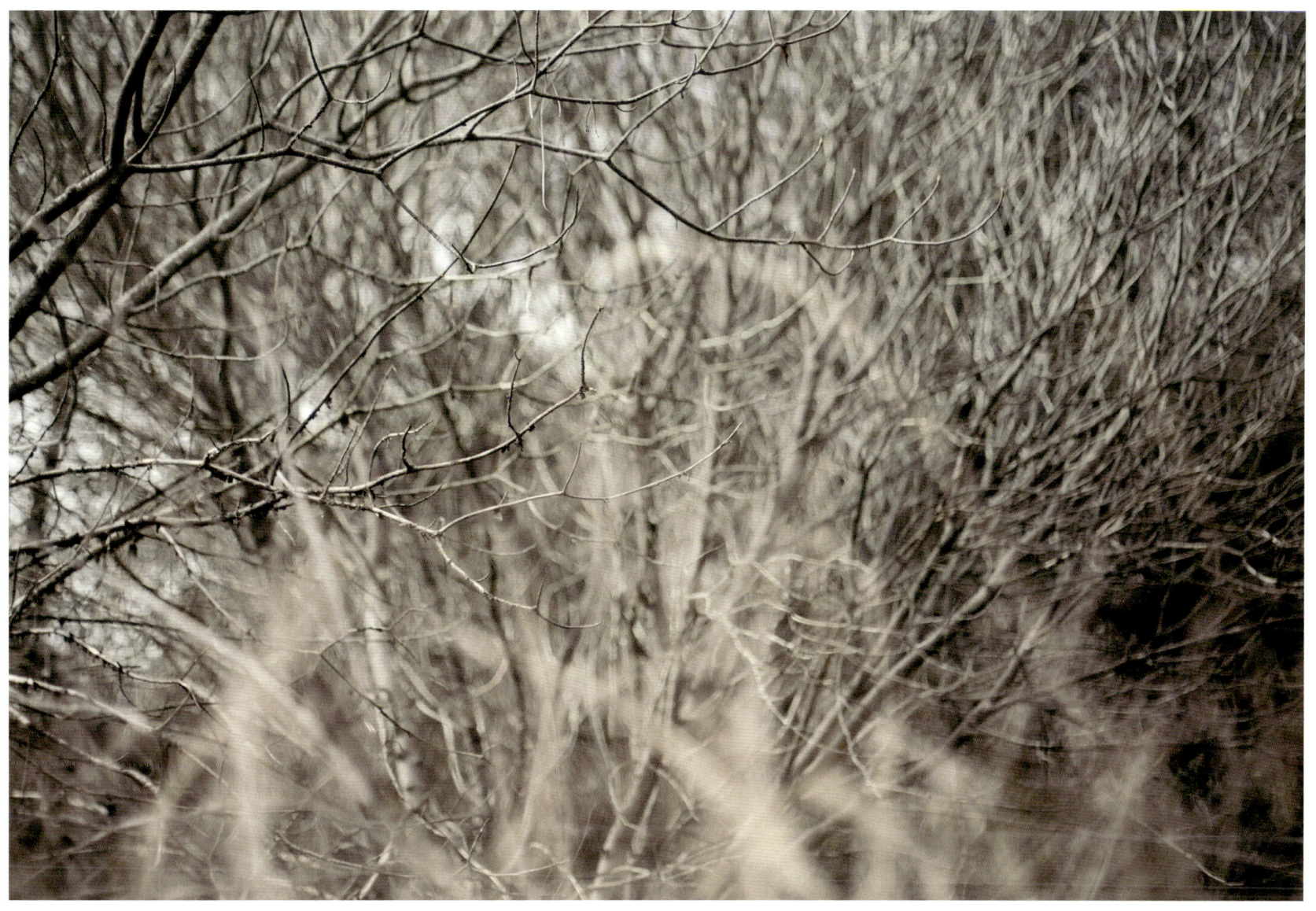

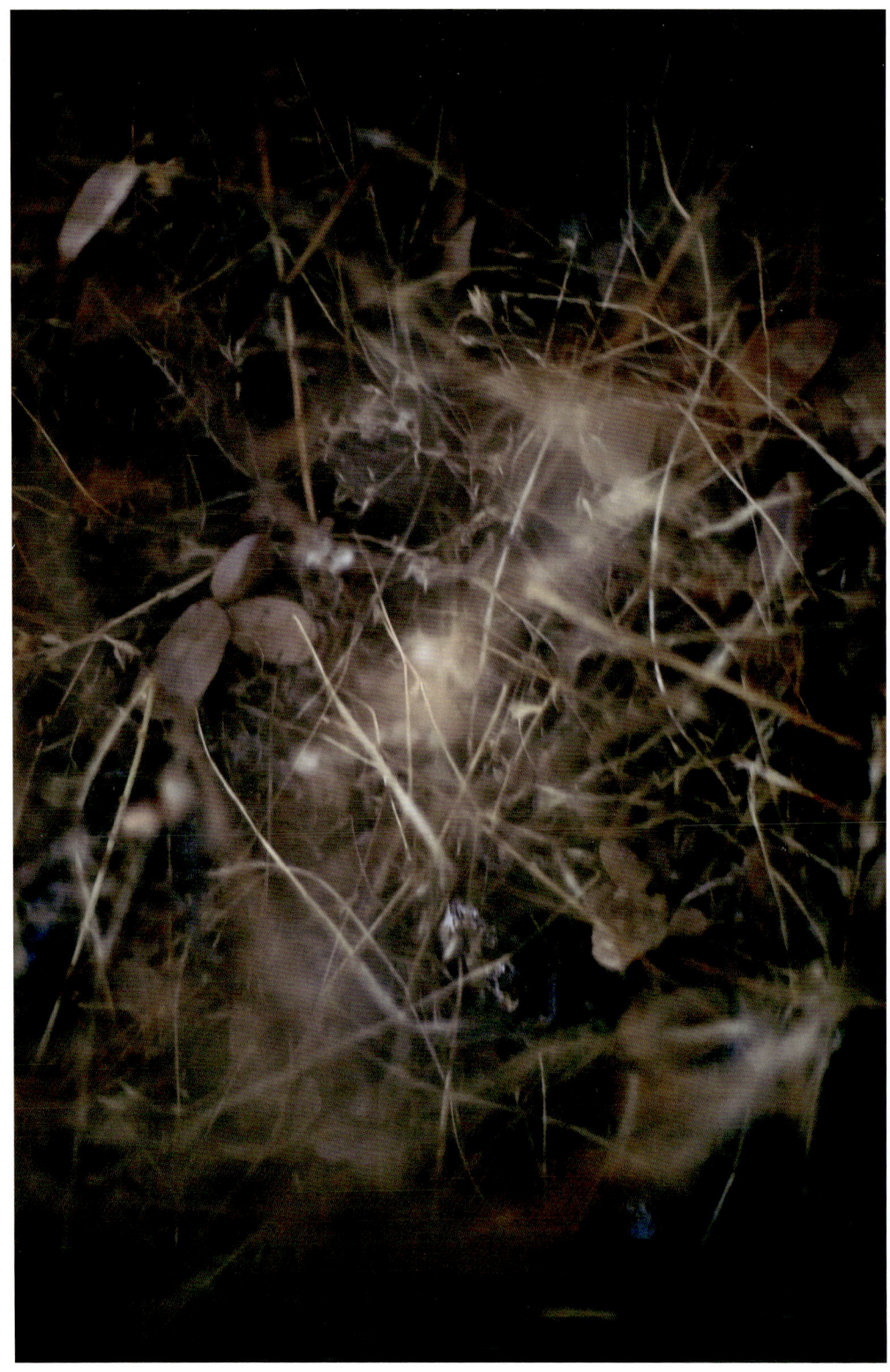

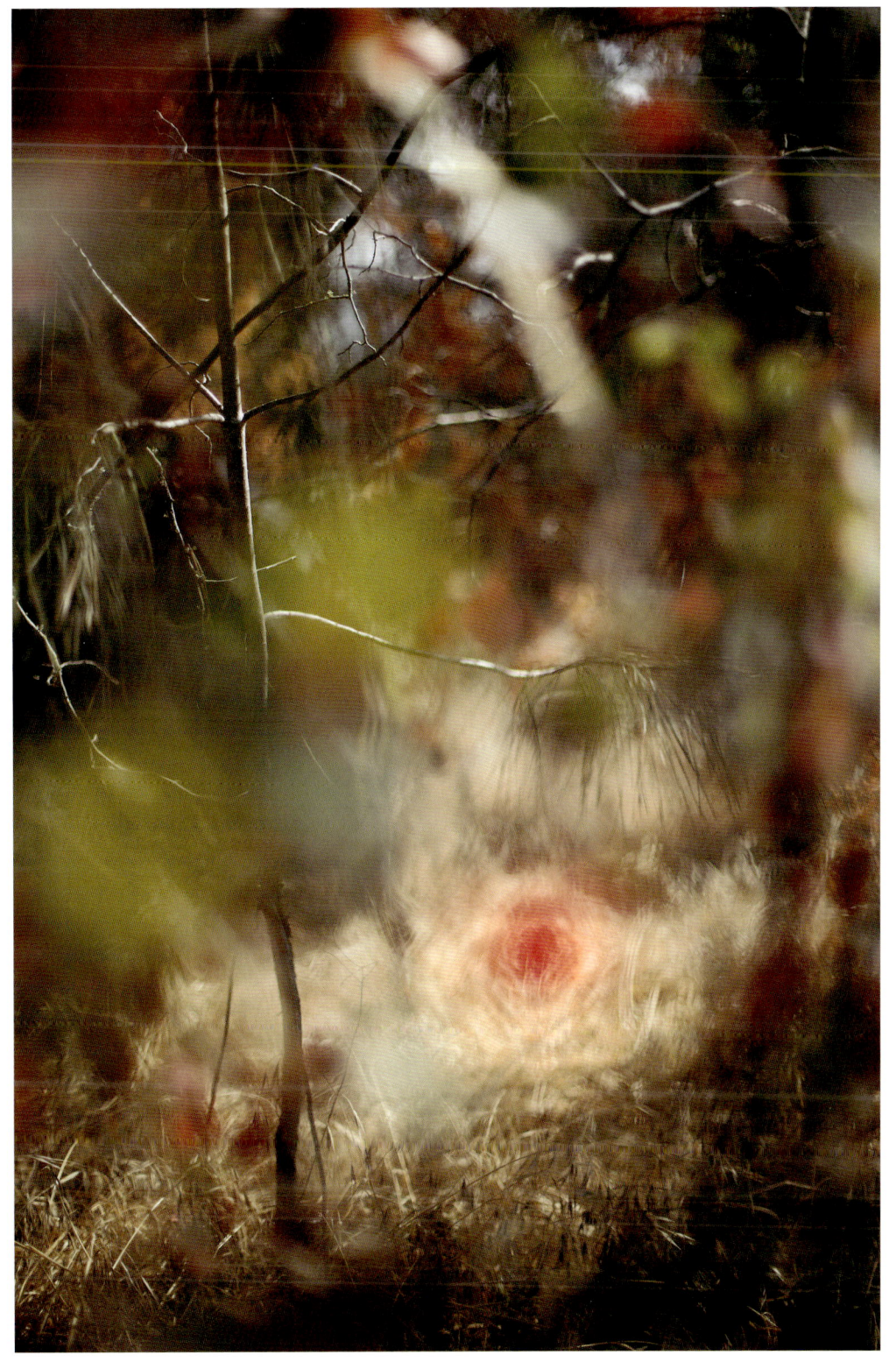

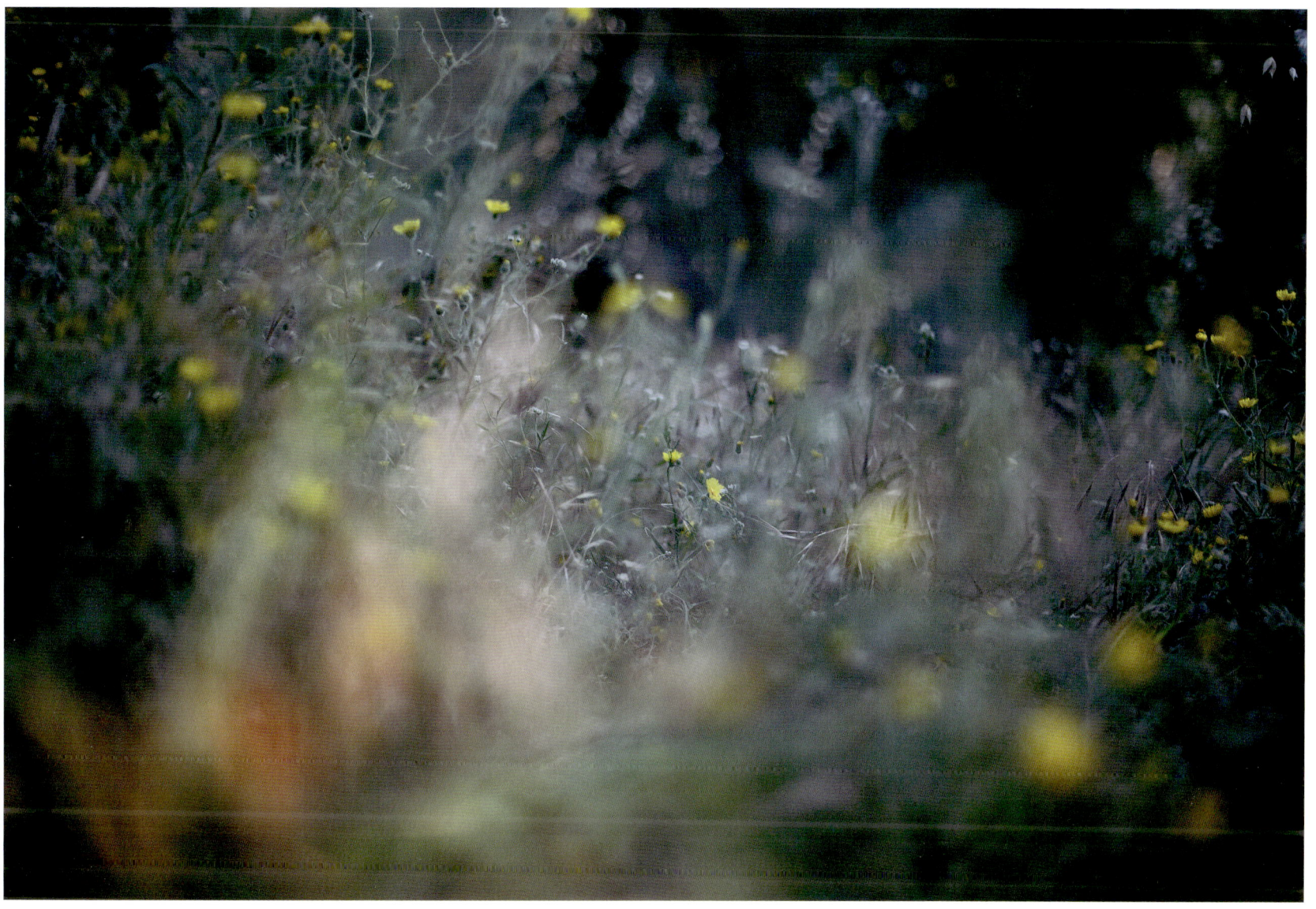

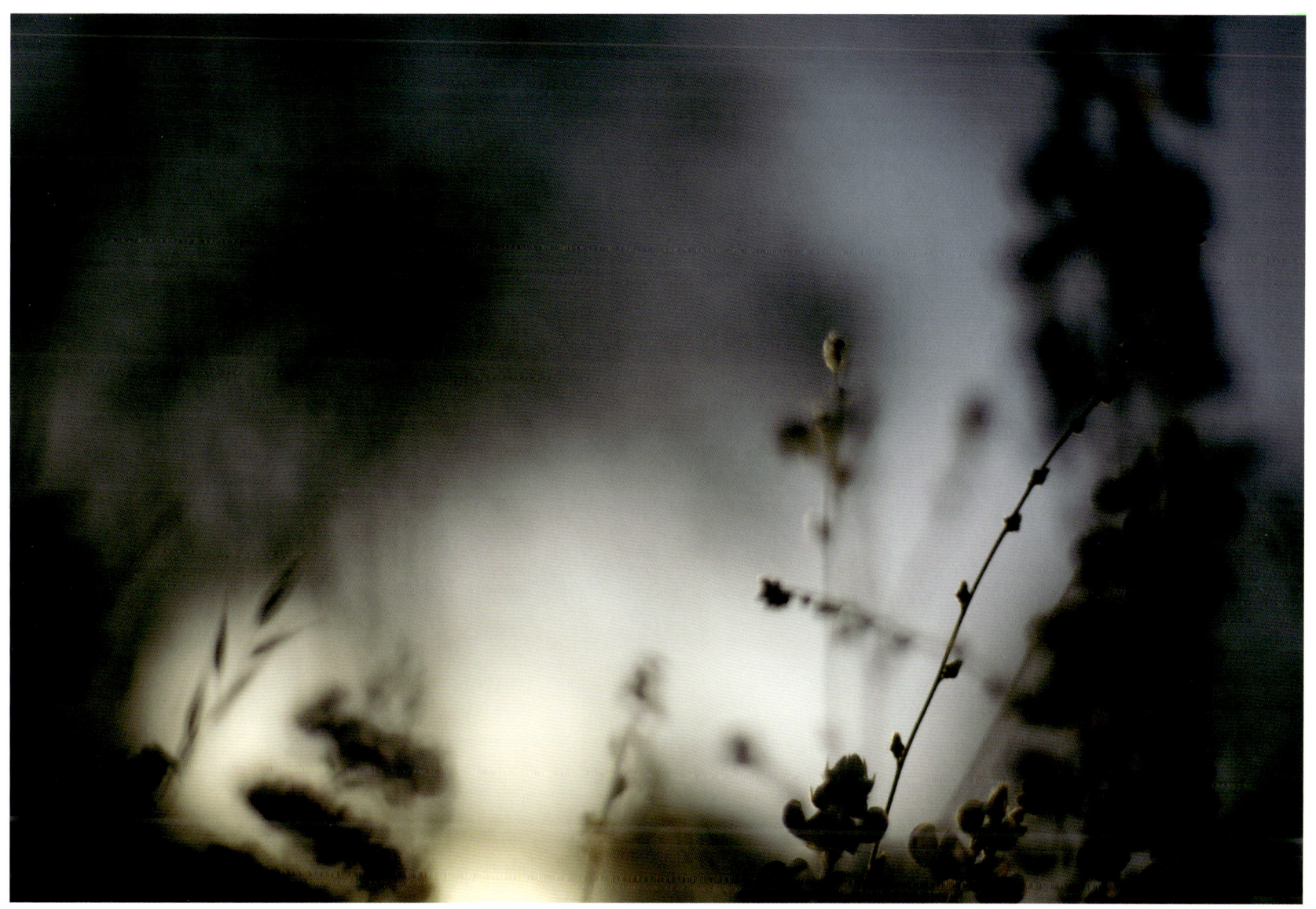

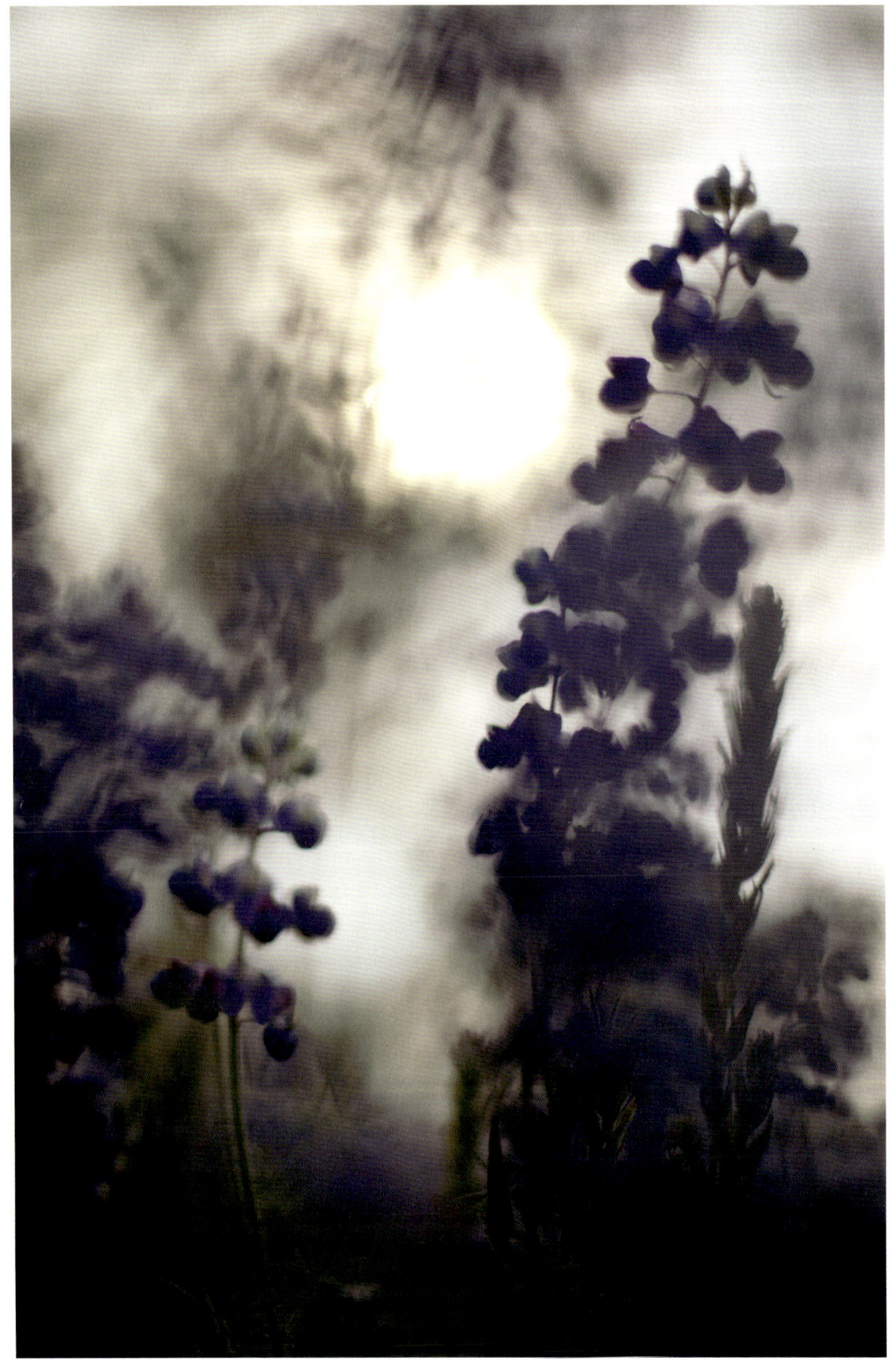

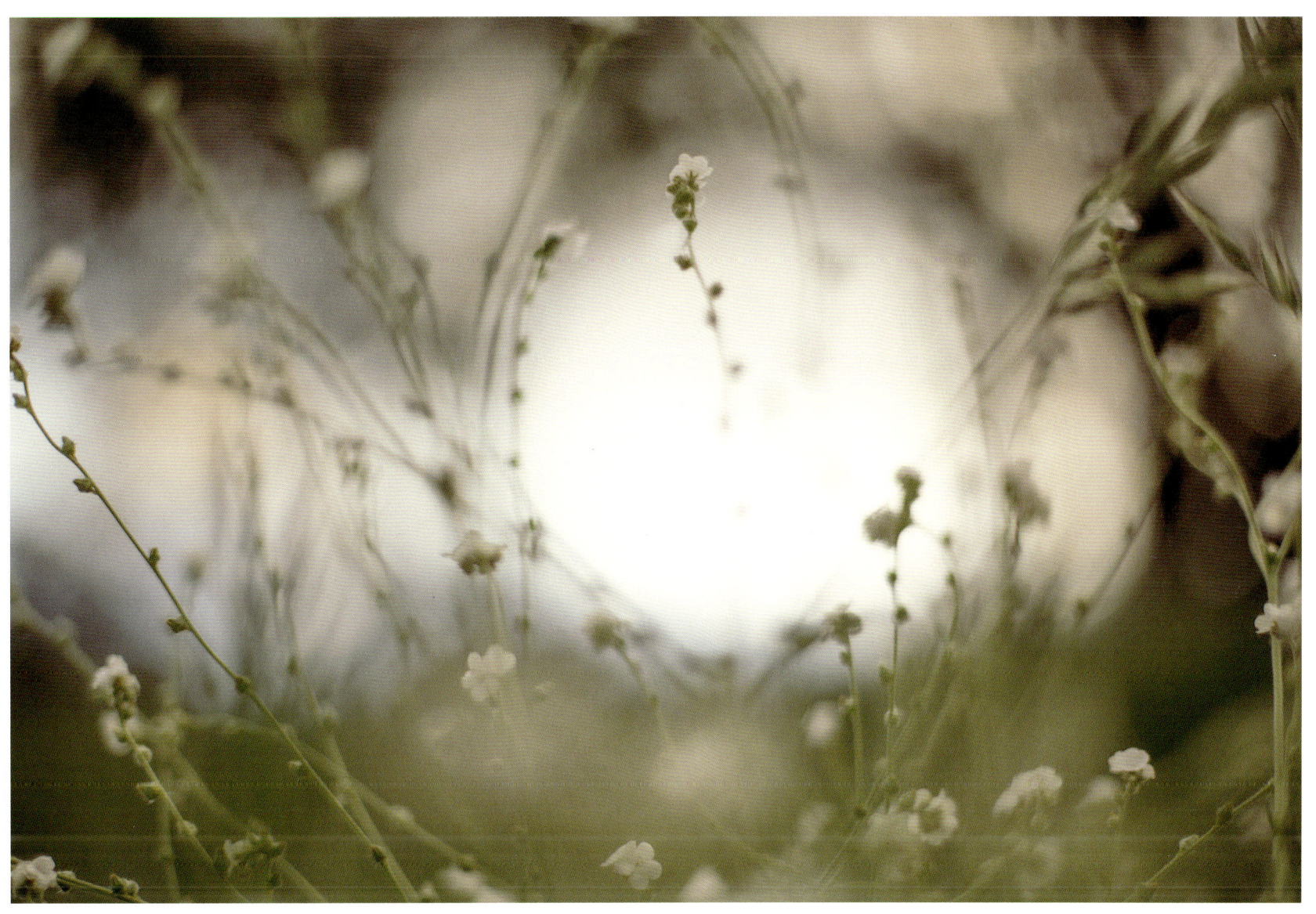

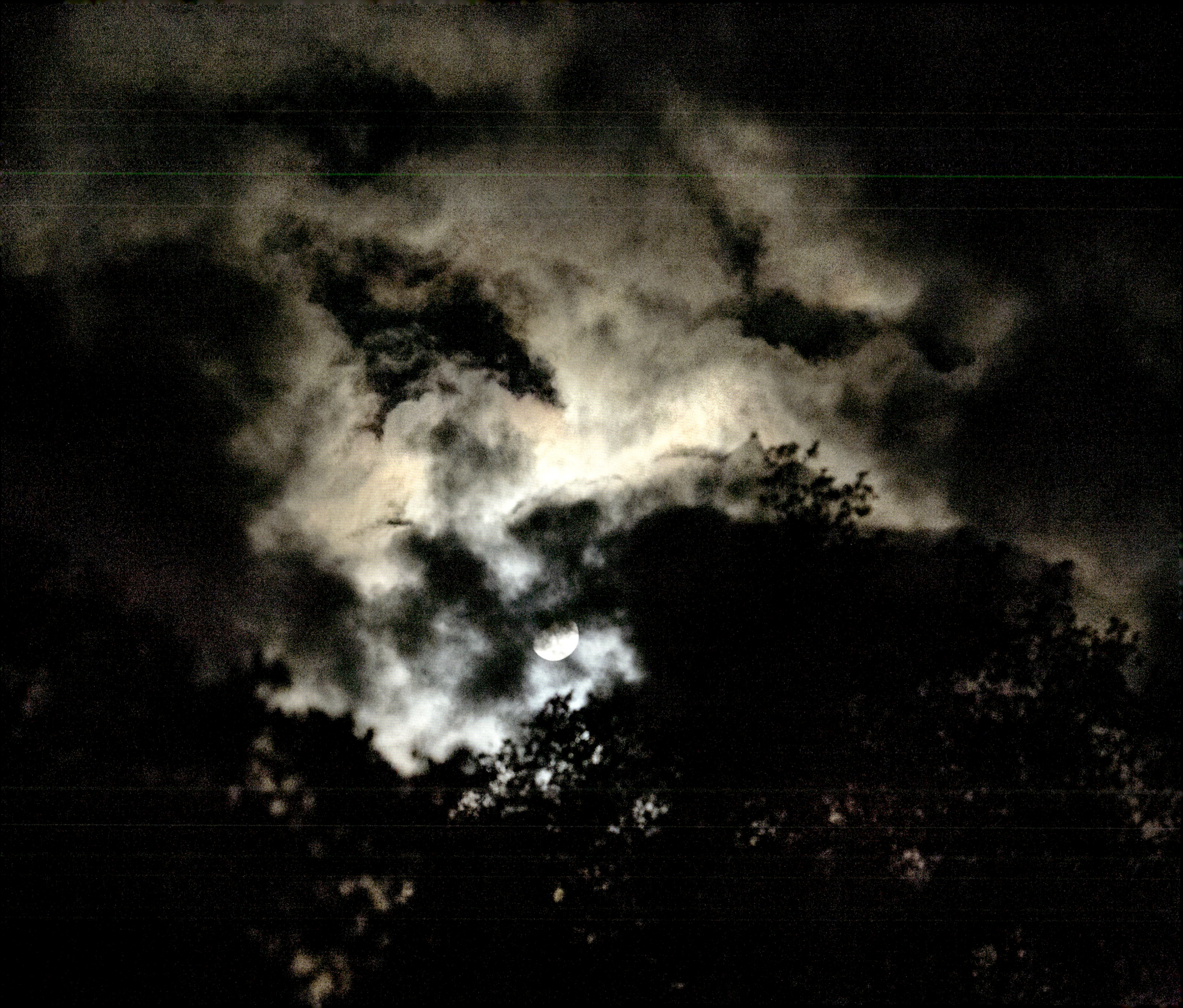

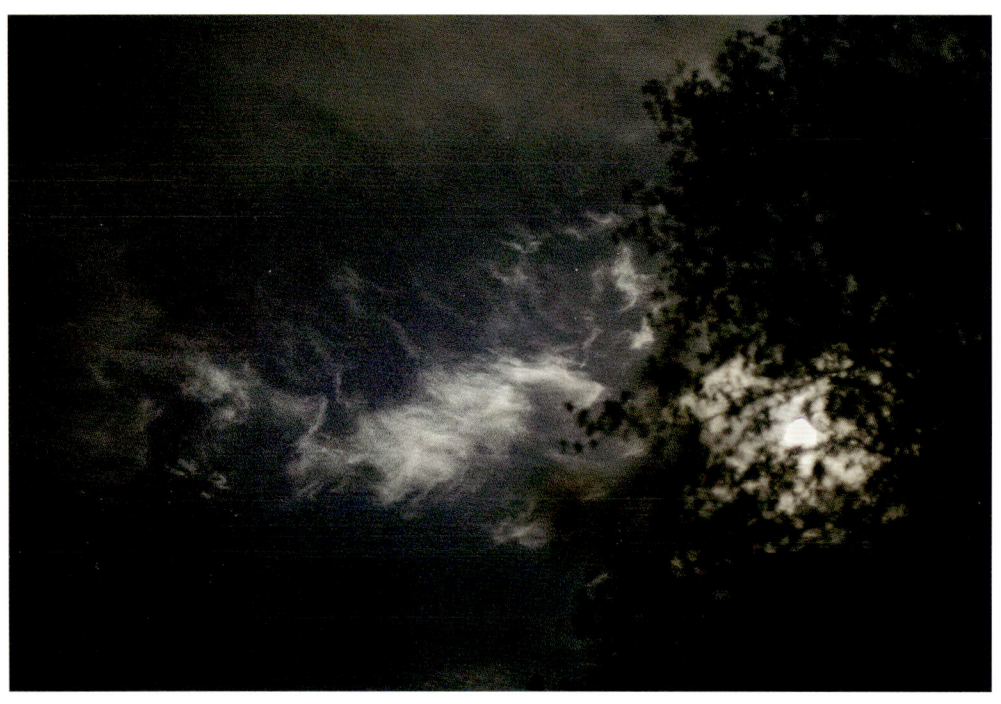

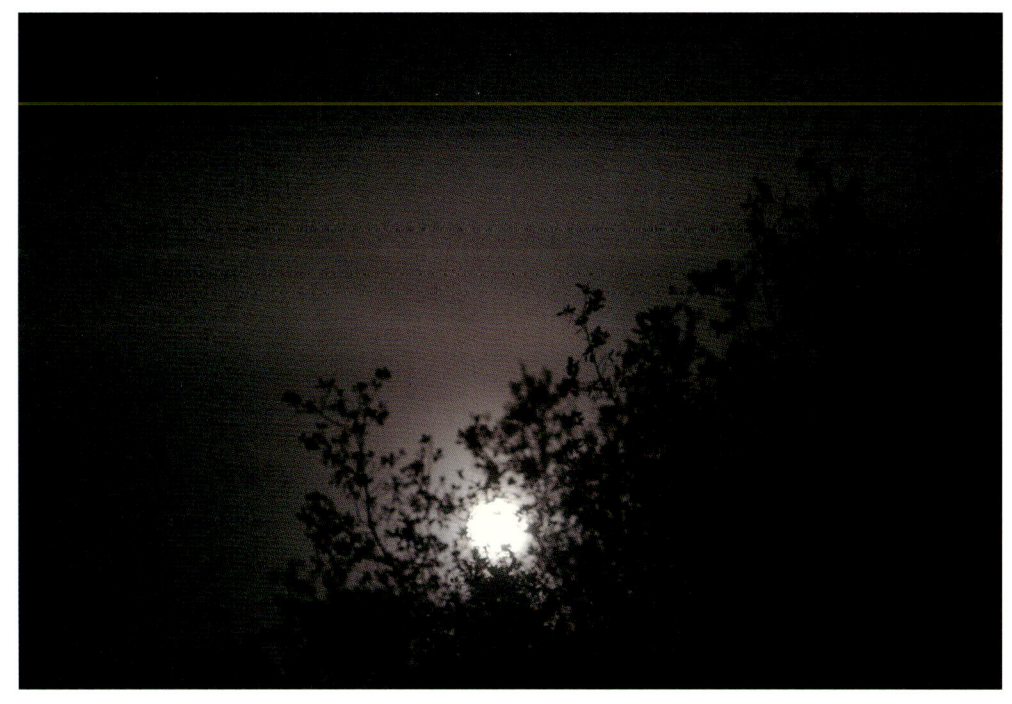

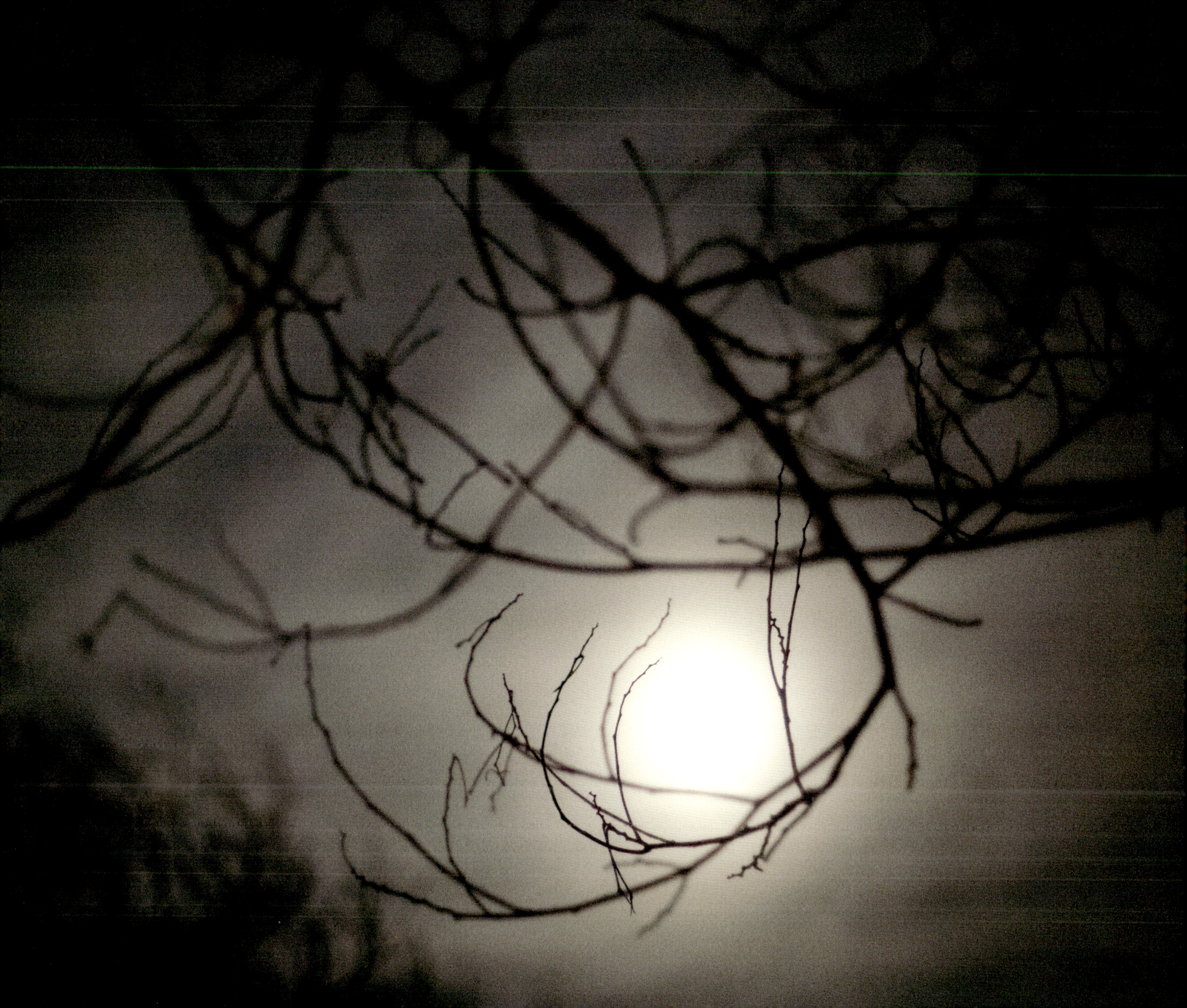

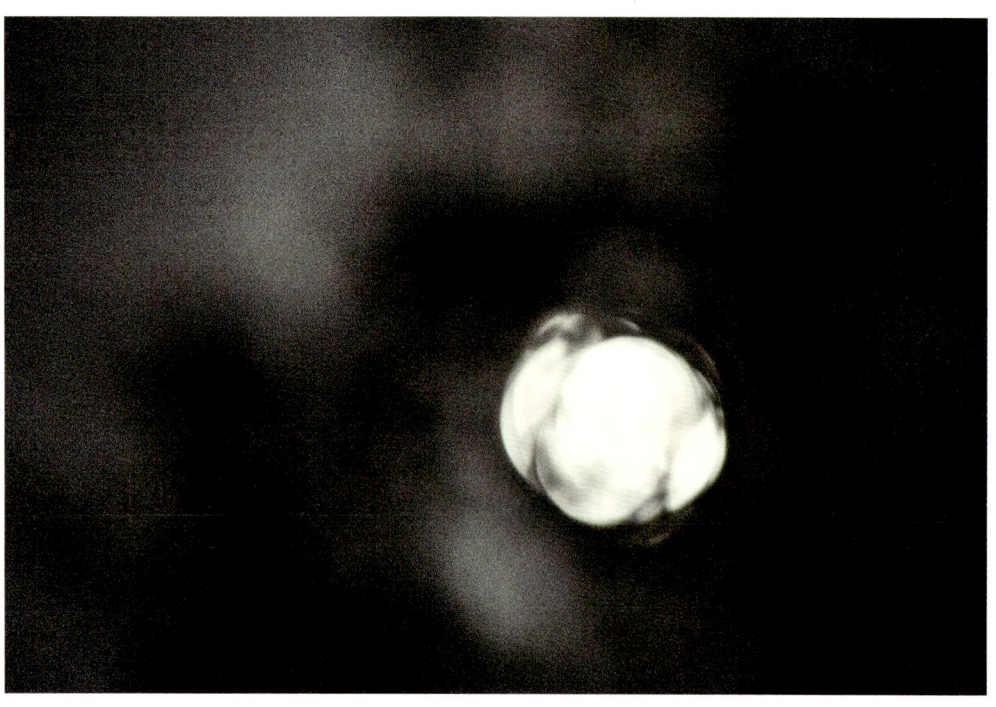

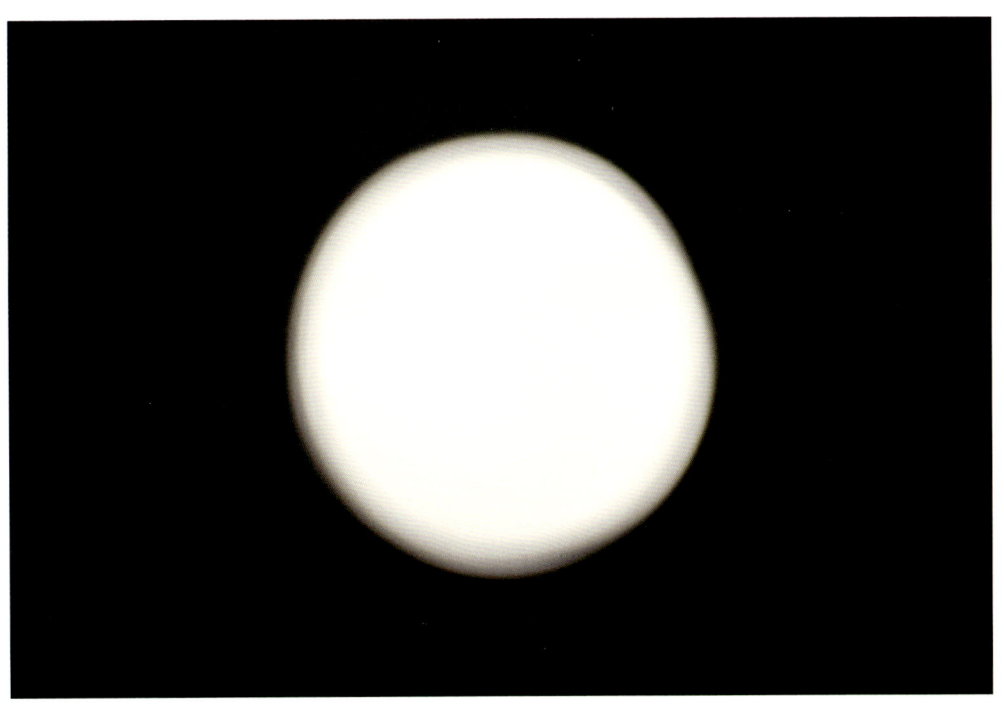

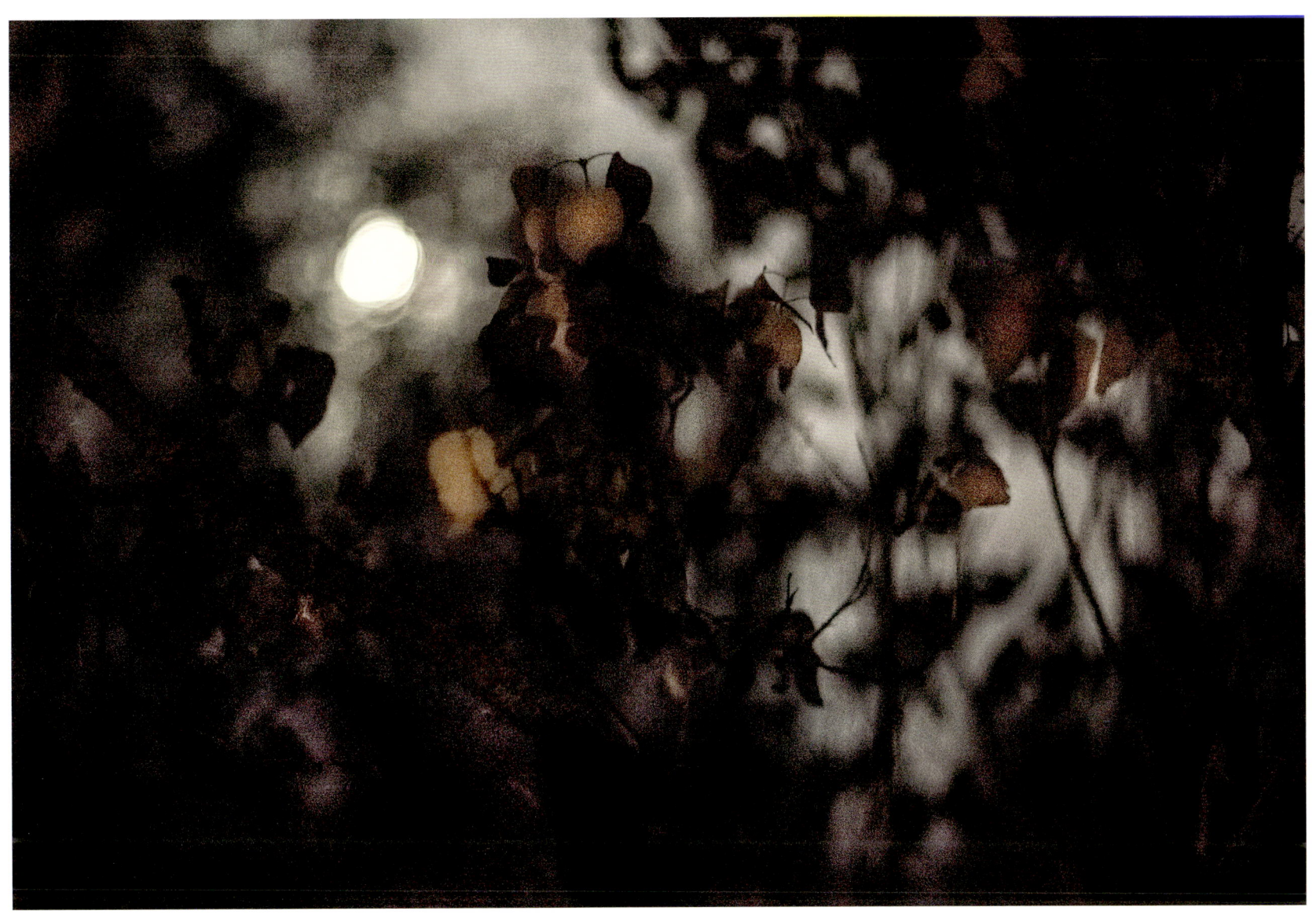

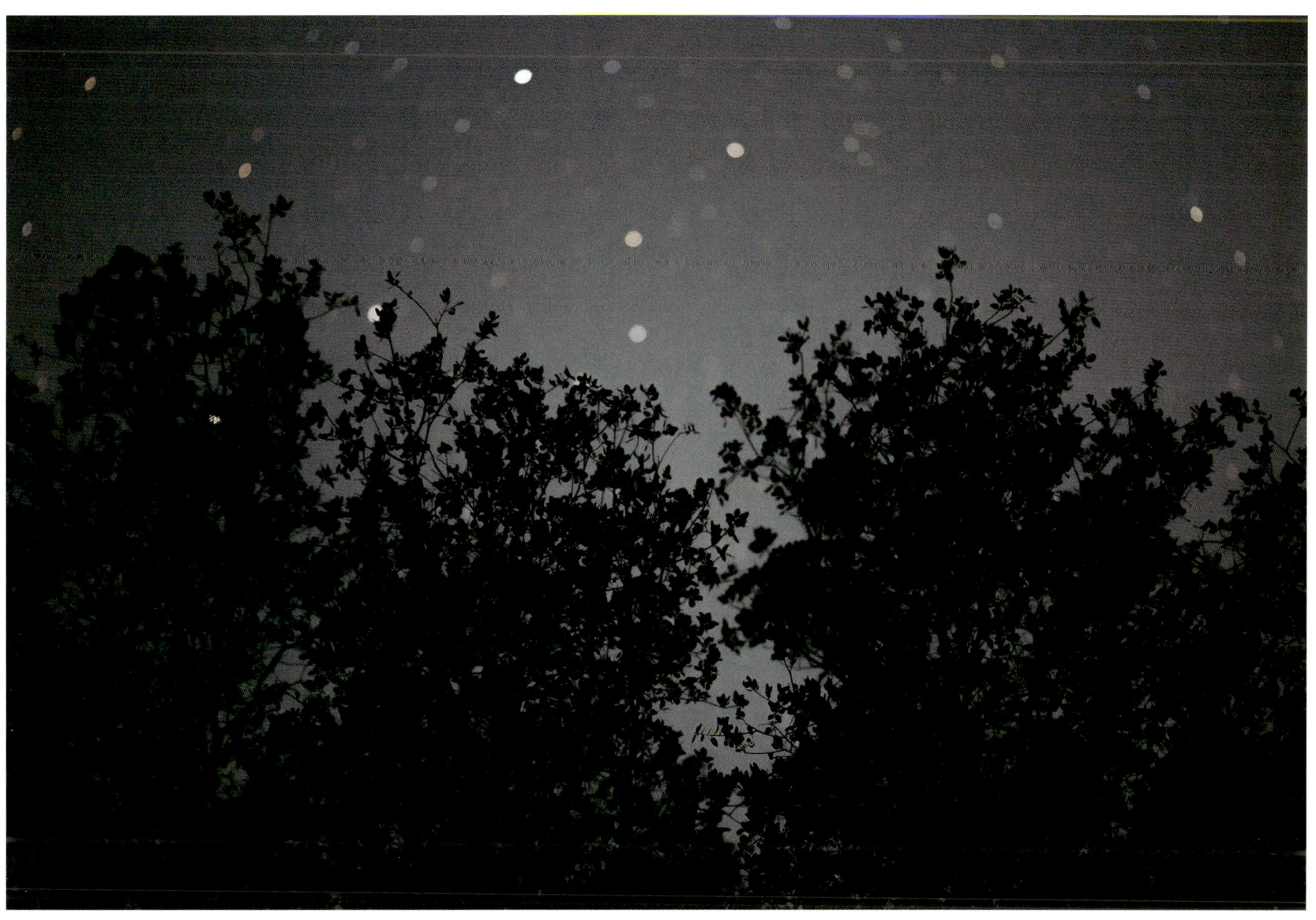

A PHOTOGRAPHIC GRACE

"There is a reality—so subtle that it becomes more real than reality. That's what I'm trying to get down in photography."
—Alfred Stieglitz

In the 20th century, the history of photography is impossible to separate from the many attempts to define and canonize what the boundaries of that history should be. Unlike other mediums before it, it came to maturity at a moment coinciding with a general meta-consciousness about art making that seemed to validate these attempts. Yet these incessant efforts to contain instead produced a fractalizing feedback loop that only revealed the morphing contours of photography and confirmed it as a medium whose center was a moving target.

In spite of the seeming elusiveness of photography, or perhaps because of it, in the fine art context of museums and galleries, lines were drawn and camps were staked out (camps that sadly still remain), perpetuating claims separated by enormous gulfs that seemed impossible for a single medium to span. Some argued that photography was merely part of a technical, optical lineage—a scientific experiment; for others it was a mystical experience (or in some cases an attempt at mystical trickery). Still others argued that its popularity and democratization indicated an end of capital, while these same characteristics led to its use as a propaganda tool for ideological repression and mass movements alike. Still others savored the individual genius that it could isolate—arguing that those who could really "see" represented a pinnacle of human aesthetic vision in its purest form.

What all these differing indexes had (and have) in common, however, is that they all prioritize human control over the visual world, a perspective that has led to—or at least abetted—a separation between the human and everything else (an irony, given that photography, like nothing before it, brought the world to us). Because the medium was forced into deep conceptual troughs from its beginning, its potential to emphasize a sense of shared wholeness was repressed. Photography was used to sanction a wedge between the (human-) seen and the (human-) unseen, enforcing a sense of dominion over the rest of the Earth, even subconsciously.

Barbara Kyne's works are healing the rifts of that long, forced separation in the most profound ways. Kyne moves with her camera through the land in Mariposa, California—not like a hunter stalking material, detached from what she seeks—but like a lucid dreamer who is, yes, more or less in control of the movements of her *camera-being* but not subject to space-time, and thus able to merge into her surroundings, becoming part of what is there.

Photography, even in its early beginnings, recognized the potential visual overlay between the dream state and ocular "reality." But Kyne's work takes advantage of that synaptic fulcrum in a completely new way that isn't simply about a visual language; because it doesn't prioritize the "human," it does not isolate us from that which is "seen." The world shifts around her hybrid *camera-being* and suggests a profound change of consciousness: What if this *is* the reality, and our millennia-long march toward developing a technology that allows this way of seeing was precisely in order to finally visibly register this as proof?

The great visionary Alfred Stieglitz had intimations of this conceptually, and his *Equivalents* series (1922–1935), in which he photographed the sky and clouds without any human boundary markers, represents one of the 20th century's heights of this exploration. Kyne is a latter-day heir to Stieglitz, and her work certainly resonates with his work and that of his two most famous lifetime protégés, Edward Steichen and Paul Strand. Something about light and mystery and texture (Steichen) and of what can be seen when human-seeing is bypassed (Strand) are here in strong force in Kyne's work.

But in this moment, there is a potential that none of those artists had: Now, the interconnectivity of the world has made previously inviolable physical boundaries moot. In the 21st century, photography, despite many people's best attempts to regulate it, like water, has found its way. The medium has proved more flexible and fluid and ubiquitous than its inventors thought possible. It is tossing off the shackles of any human-imposed definition. In our mediated world, photography is now practically boundaryless, and we are following *its* lead.

Barbara Kyne is very much a 21st-century photographer, and when we see in her photographs that the trees are dancing, that the light has material form and is communicating very distinctly with the plant life it serves, and that darkness is a passageway and an invitation from the natural world, we can trust that this is not anthropomorphizing because her *camera-being* perspective eschews any separation between us and Earth. And what she brings back through her photographs is evidence of a different, far more thrilling reality: We are part of a magical universe that beckons us to return.

In this way, Kyne's photographs represent a grace, a vision that is nothing short of a vision of God.

Jasmine Moorhead
Oakland, California, 2016

ON SENTIENCE AND REALITY

This body of work, created between March 2013 and April 2016, imagines what the consciousness of plants might be. What do they know? How do they feel? How do they interact with other species? In *A Crack in the World* I focus on the five acres of nature entrusted to my partner and me. The acreage is not far from the small town of Mariposa in the magical foothills of the Sierra Nevada mountain range in California, a town named for the monarch butterflies that return there in spring after overwintering in Mexico. There is something mystical about this land that compels me to engage with it, to ask: *What is the nature of reality?*

I am trying to pierce reality for myself and for the viewer. I'm not looking for magic *out there*, but from a worldview that collapses the dualism between science and religion. While we can allow that science has not even imagined the nature of reality and has a tendency toward reductionism, can we also admit that the dictates of various theologies might come from texts intended to be allegorical? In fact, that the contradictory nature of these texts practically demands it?

I propose that phenomena do not defy the laws of the universe, that all phenomena are subject to science. We just don't know its rules yet, and may never know them. We can study them in many ways, though, such as in the feedback loop that is the artistic process. We have an idea, we explore it, receive feedback from the exploration, refine or modify the idea and explore it again, on and on until we've satisfied something for ourselves or moved on to another question. In the creative process, art is a byproduct of that interaction.[1]

I approach the question of reality as if the camera and I are a unique species that sees as only *it* can. We (the camera and I) explore, and wonder what is outside of our *umwelt*, a concept introduced by biologist Jakob von Uexküll

in 1909: Different species use their senses to define their environs, their *umwelt*, naturally assuming that reality is what they perceive with their senses.[2] In the case of humans, we think reality is what we can perceive, measure with our instruments, and comprehend based on our scientific knowledge, or what our religious institutions tell us—and all of these, taken as dogma, limit us infinitely from knowing the Universe. They exclude the unsensed and unimagined.

Perhaps perception with our senses is the biggest obstacle to knowing reality, since it is an unconscious bias. Phenomena are explained through the senses. For example, the visual system in the human is 10 percent eyes and 90 percent neurological networks. When we dream, we are hallucinating 100 percent of the time, and we may be hallucinating much of the time we're awake, as well. What is considered real is subjective in the sense that it is agreed upon by the individual or group that is doing the perceiving.[3] Interpretations differ.

What we see and hear *really does seem real*, and may be, but is only a fraction of what *IS*. Cosmologists and astrophysicists are confidently theorizing extra dimensions in which we might be a tiny speck within a three-dimensional universe that is itself enveloped in a larger-dimensioned universe, or in a parallel universe from which we can't perceive other universes. At the very least, physicists now tend to agree that time and space are probably illusions.[4]

Much has been discovered about the consciousness of plants and their senses in the past two decades. Neurobiologist Stefano Mancuso enumerates their abilities in *Brilliant Green: The Surprising History and Science of Plant Intelligence.* Mancuso outlines 15 senses plants have (that we know of), in addition to possessing the five human ones (that we comprehend).

They communicate, remember, learn, and solve problems. They are even self-conscious, in that they can recognize and distinguish themselves from other plants. They photosynthesize, and if they didn't, humans could not have evolved or even now live on this planet. Finally, plants operate more like a network, suggesting a possible 21st-century model for human survival.[5] What if plants are even more intelligent than humans and know more about reality than we do?

Created in-camera and processed with only the usual color and density adjustments, these photographs are sensory artifacts that offer a conduit through which the viewer may experience this expanded perception of the natural world. They are part abstract and part representational, emphasizing what is overlooked, underlying, and even undetected by our five human senses. Still, at times they seem more real than what we normally perceive, and perhaps there is a species that sees somewhat like this. Naturally, such a species would define reality by *its* sentience.

As the project progresses, it becomes indisputable to me that we are of nature and not separate from it. Like the dancing trees and seeking plants, we resemble other species, we act like them, we experience joy and suffering as they do. The sentience of all living entities and our shared consciousness jumps out at me as I peer through what seems like a crack in the world that allows me to begin to perceive some of its secrets. Orbs pop, and streaks of light dance through the layered dimensions of land and sky. Perception shifts as the small becomes outsize and the distant alive. I observe the cycles of life, death, and rebirth and am struck by the inextricable connection between pathos and joy. The images evoke delight, warmth, awe, fear, and discomfort, sometimes all in the same photograph. I hope they invite empathy for nature in the viewer. Perhaps if we had more empathy, we would take better care.

Unlike the human sphere, nature has no hierarchy of importance or beauty. We don't know as much about dirt as the grass does, nor about pollen as the bee, and are only beginning to discover how the monarch butterflies that land *en masse* like a carpet at my home in Mariposa might navigate their way back from Mexico every year. Yet from the complex to the simple, everything is equally vital, is connected—is one.

This direct conduit to another species' reality may create an awareness that we can't possibly fully understand each other or the world we live in, so would be wise to operate with less intellectual arrogance and more humility. With crises such as global warming and ecocide looming, we need to find solutions. Empathy for each other and for the planet that sustains us could be the vital first step.

Barbara Kyne
Oakland, California, 2016

1 The idea of art as a byproduct of the creative process was expressed in conversation to me by my friend and fellow artist Geri Donovan.

2 Jakob von Uexküll, *Theoretical Biology* (Harcourt, Brace, 1926).

3 David Eagleman, *Incognito: The Secret Lives of the Brain* (Vintage, 2011)

4 Lisa Randall, *Warped Passages* (HarperCollins, 2005).

5 Stefano Mancuso and Alessandra Viola, *Brilliant Green: The Surprising History and Science of Plant Intelligence*, trans. Joan Benham (Island Press, 2015).

INDEX

ACKNOWLEDGMENTS

When I told my father, John, that I wanted to study photography instead of law, he said, "Why don't you go to law school first?" Thanks to Dad for relenting and sticking with me through grad school and beyond, and for telling me ever since I can remember that I could do anything I wanted to. He is missed. To my mother, Barbara for her warmth, wisdom, and prized sense of humor. And her name. Thank you to my siblings, Michael, Eileen, Diane, Douglas, and Chris, for their various qualities of intelligence, creativity, fierceness, gentleness, loyalty, and especially for their love and humor. To my nieces and nephews, Jordan, Lazar, Aleksandra, Natalija, and Stefan Nikolic, who fill our lives with joy. And to their father, Dusko, who partnered with my sister Diane, bestowing his comedy, style, charisma, and handsomeness DNA to the family. Thanks to the Bornemanns for their excellent cousin-ness. Special thanks to Gram, Matilda Murray, who passed away last year at 106 years of age. She was a lonely, hungry orphan, always with enough love for her family of 34 and counting. I inherited her love of the *New York Times* Sunday crossword but would never play her in Scrabble. She cheated. To Kelly, Lucy, Baron, and Trapper for all the fun and games with string and balls, except Kelly who might have given me parvovirus because she loved to scratch our bare feet as we ran up and down the stairs.

Thanks to the talented people at Daylight Books. To the publisher and cofounder Michael Itkoff, who chose the project and believed in it. To designer Ursula Damm, whose kindness and patience with me was heartening when the work ahead seemed daunting. To Daylight's copy editor, Elizabeth Bell, who tidied up the erratatas.

Through the years, as I read the brilliant Pulitzer-nominated writer Susan Griffin, I would never have thought that she would be so generous as to write a forward for a book of mine. Dreams do come true. Thank you beyond words to Griffin for a poetic and powerful introduction and for allowing herself to see and be seduced. And thank you for writing those books! If I were a writer, I would want to be Susan Griffin.

I first saw curator Jasmine Moorhead of Krowswork in a panel discussion at an art event in San Francisco, a few years prior to the making of this book. The minute she opened her mouth, I said to myself, "HER!" I count myself truly fortunate to collaborate with Moorhead on this book, as she sees the potential of photography as I do, and expresses it with piercing intelligence and authority (and because she uses my name in the same breath as Stieglitz, Steichen, and Strand). Big thanks also for the editing and sequencing assist.

To my longtime mentors and friends Colleen Ringrose and Geri Donovan, thank you for your encouragement and for reminding me who I am. To Beth Benson for championing this body of work when it was coming together. And to Hiroshi Sugimoto, Bill Jacobson, and Andy Goldsworthy for being artists.

Unending thanks to my love, Fran Lowe, whose *umwelt* I choose to share before all others and who makes it all possible.